HIGH NOON

HIGH NOON

Twenty Global Problems, Twenty Years to Solve Them

J. F. RISCHARD

Viva Books Private Limited

New Delhi • Mumbai • Chennai • Kolkata • Bangalore

First Indian Edition 2004

VIVA BOOKS PRIVATE LIMITED

- 4262/3 Ansari Road, Daryaganj, New Delhi 110 002
  E-mail: viva@vivagroupindia.net
- 215-216 New Apollo Estate, 2nd Floor, Mogra Lane, Andheri (E),
  Mumbai 400 069 E-mail: vivamumbai@vivagroupindia.net
- 7 Aziz Mulk, Seventh Street, Thousand Lights, Chennai 600 006
  E-mail: vivachennai@vivagroupindia.net
- B–103, Jindal Towers, 21/1A/3, Darga Road, Kolkata 700 017
  E-mail: vivakolkata@vivagroupindia.net
- 7 Sovereign Park Apts., 56-58 K. R. Road, Basavanagudi,
  Bangalore 560 004 Email: vivabangalore@vivagroupindia.net

Visit us at *www.vivagroupindia.com*

Published by arrangement with

Basic Books
A Member of the Perseus Books Group
387 Park Avenue South
New York, NY 10016-8810

ISBN 81-7649-621-9

Published by Vinod Vasishtha for Viva Books Private Limited, 4262/3 Ansari Road, Daryaganj, New Delhi 110 002 and printed & bound at Raj Press, R-3 Inderpuri, New Delhi – 110012.

For Anthony, Christopher, and Alexandre

Contents

Author's Note and Warning

This is not another book on globalization. In fact, before my publisher pushed me to call it *High Noon*, I had my heart set on *It's Not Globalization, Stupid.*

Why take a swipe at globalization? Because like all mushy concepts, it confuses rather than enlightens. Many people tend to relate it only to economic items, like world trade and capital flows, when there clearly are some other big things going on—such as the planet's population going from 5 billion a decade ago to about 8 billion less than a generation from now. Worse, some people imagine that globalization is dark-suited men getting together every Monday morning in Washington or New York to decide how best to make money by degrading the environment and promoting poverty and distress throughout the world. More innocently, most people mix up two things: global changes and the failure to respond correctly to them.

So wherever you turn, you'll see that the concept of globalization brings about a mild paralysis of the brain. It leads to misdiagnoses, witch-hunts, and spectacular misunderstandings. And as the debate gets muddled, we all end up distracted from one of the most pressing challenges on this planet: global problem-solving. If we needed a reminder of how urgent that particular challenge is, the events of September 11, 2001, provided it.

The objective of this short book is to instill clarity into today's debates. In doing so, my vantage point won't be that of the official from the World Bank I happen to be, but that of a concerned global citizen who is in a position to see quite a few things from his lookout post. (Needless to say, the views I express in this highly personal book are my own, not those of the institution I belong to.)

To achieve this objective, I save you 100 pages right off the bat by sparing you the usual made-up anecdotes ("As he glanced at the latest Korean reserves figures, Larry Summers started sweating profusely" or "The sun was already setting over the Santa Fe Institute when the fax started spewing out the climate change report"). Instead, I use graphs that serve as maps and provide structure—and make that structure come alive through examples of what's going on. I'd rather come across as pedantic than verbose.

And I will sail closer to the risk of oversimplification than of excessive detail. As a practitioner and generalist, I get a lot of my information and conceptual background from live discussions on my ideas and those of others with leaders and audiences from all over the world. But unlike specialized research types, I may have an advantage in putting things together into some sort of big picture, and that's exactly what I'll try to do.

As I do this, I'll be somewhat polemical. As someone said: if you haven't got an edge, you haven't got a point.

The Book Has Three Parts

The first part deals with *explanation*. It provides the context. Its message: forget about globalization. Instead of one shapeless force, think of *two* big forces that will produce spectacular worldwide changes over the next twenty years: a sizeable population increase on an already overstretched planet, and the intensely different new world economy that's emerging. And think of three new realities that will affect human institutions as they try to adapt to these two forces—the move away from hierarchies, the struggles of the nation-state, and the blurring of the boundary lines between the public sector, business, and civil society. To get even with my publisher, I use my old, somewhat obnoxious title, *It's Not Globalization, Stupid,* for that part.

The second part of the book is about *documentation.* Its main message is that in the context of the two big forces, there are twenty or so big and burning global issues that need to be resolved well before twenty years are over. I took a deep breath and wrote them all up in about three pages each—to give you a pretty good overview without drowning you, and myself, in details. That is really the *High Noon* part—named after the Gary Cooper Western in which a tense community anxiously awaits a showdown set for noon, while the clock ticks off minutes that are both long and terribly short.

The third part is about a badly needed form of *speculation* I would like to engage you in. The current international setup isn't delivering solutions to these urgent global issues fast enough, if at all. Yet we cannot have a global government. What other options are there for serious, accelerated global problem-solving? What can we do to preserve our small planet before it's too late? This is the *Thinking Aloud* part, in which I will be trying to offer novel ideas, at some risk to myself.

Not exactly cheerful stuff, you'll say. But deep down this is a very optimistic book. It says that traditional thinking won't do. Nation-states are struggling. International institutions are in the doghouse. Politicians, with their short electoral horizons and their territorial bent, aren't about to produce solutions to urgent global issues. Nor will protesters, whose tendency to see nonexistent plots often impedes their search for solutions—in fact, they have offered few so far.

The problem is that most of the players tend to think along traditional, obsolete lines. But there is much we can do if we think *differently*, borrowing concepts from the new world of networks. Some of the ideas I present will look radical, even naive. But the real naïveté may be elsewhere—in the belief that business as usual will take care of things. It won't.

Two Ways to Read This Book

I have kept this book short in the hope you can read it in one or two sittings. Yet there's a second way to read it:

- skip chapters 12, 13, and 14—which give details on each of the twenty global issues

- get the main story line in only half the book's total number of pages

- then, if you like, return to the details on the issues

Both ways work, but I recommend the second approach only to more hurried readers. Whatever you do, however, don't skip Part One, even if you think you know it all—or you won't get the full meaning of Part Three.

PART ONE

It's Not Globalization, Stupid

1
Two Big Forces

Over the next twenty years, two big forces will deeply change the world as we know it. Indeed, the rate of change will be unprecedented.

Just think: by 2020, not long from now, China could be well on its way to becoming once again the world's largest economy, some 200 years after losing the title. Billions of computer chips will have launched a world in which objects talk to each other. Electronic money will have sent central banks scrambling for new roles. Water will have replaced petroleum as a main cause of strategic tension.

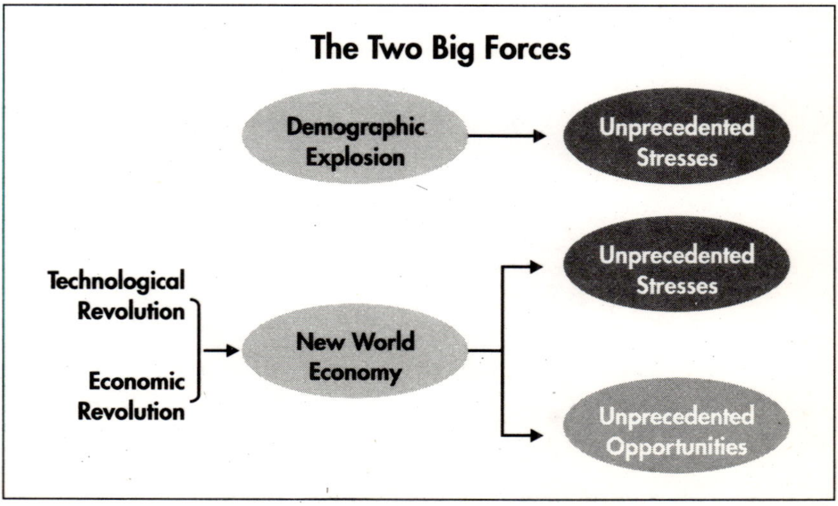

FIGURE 1.1 *The Two Big Forces*

All in all, the next twenty years could bring more rapid and more profound change than any other period in history.

The first force behind this coming period of intense change, which I'll refer to as the demographic explosion, brings only stresses. The second force, the new world economy, brings a mixture of stresses and opportunities. Figure 1.1 offers a simple, self-explanatory framework. It is the map for the next few chapters.

2

Stretching the Planet to the Limit: The Demographic Explosion

The demographic force can be described in one short sentence: we will go from an already overstretched planet of 5 billion people in 1990 and 6 billion people today to about 8 billion by 2020–2025—in less than one generation.[1]

The good news is that after that, the planet's population will either stagnate or, even if it grows some more, reach a plateau at around 9–10 billion in the second part of this century, after which it may even decline.[2] About fifteen years ago, forecasters fretted about much more worrisome scenarios. Happily, they were wrong. Some experts may therefore feel that I am overdoing it a bit when I talk about an explosion.

But consider the bad news: like a locomotive, global population growth requires a long braking period before it comes to a halt. In other words, there's nothing one can do about this increase to 8 billion. The people who will have these children are, for the most part, already or about to be born. And this figure does reflect the recent and ongoing decline in birth rates in much of the developing world. At any rate, this increase of about 2 billion over today's population, coming to a planet that is already overstretched, will act and feel like an explosion sending ripples into various directions.

Some readers may still resent my use of the term "demographic explosion," which has become politically incorrect. To those I would respond that I'm not a Cassandra or even a Malthusian, but that the resources and living space of the planet will be far more stretched with 8 billion people a few short decades from now than with 5 billion in 1990, let alone only 3 billion in 1960. Just consider the following dozen implications.

More than 95 percent of the 2 billion people to be added over the next two decades or so will live in developing countries. Most will keep flocking to the *cities,* producing in 2020 a world where more than one person in two lives in a city. There will be some sixty cities with more than 5 million inhabitants (almost double their number in 1990), and perhaps twenty-five huge agglomerations of 10 million and more people (up from fewer than ten in 1990).[3]

Karachi, São Paulo, and Dhaka will hover at around 20 million. Asian-style urban overcrowding and congestion will become a regular feature across the globe, with many negative consequences for poverty, health, and social stresses. Imagine the challenges of traffic, housing, waste management, sewage, and water supply in these sprawling cities. Even Africa will face ever-increasing urbanization rates, averaging 50 percent by 2020, double the level of a generation ago.

With this population increase and with higher living standards in developing countries, the world's *food production* will have to increase by 40 percent over the next twenty years. Cereal consumption may rise by 30 percent, and meat consumption by 60 percent. Some people even forecast higher increases. In any case, even if most people agree that there's no risk that the world won't be able to feed itself overall, getting there will be a tall order. It's becoming very hard to expand arable land, and the growth of crop yields will slow—in part because soils are rapidly becoming eroded or ruined by salt deposits. In many places, the limits of ever more intensive agriculture have become ominously clear. Declining underground water levels and nitrate pollution by fertilizers are just two frequent symptoms, in rich and poor countries alike.[4]

Similarly, *energy* consumption will rise to the point where, in 2020, the developing world may be close to overtaking the rich countries in

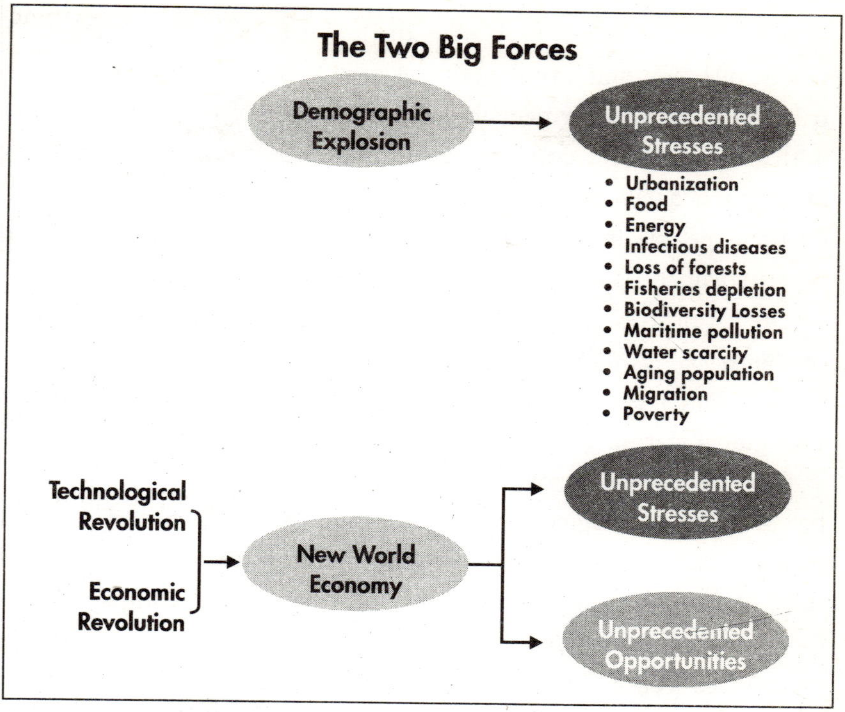

FIGURE 2.1 *Demographic Explosion—Unprecedented Stresses*

total carbon emissions from burning oil, gas, coal, and wood. Overall energy consumption will be close to double what it is now, even triple in many developing countries. In some, power production could rise fivefold.

While there's not the slightest risk that the world will run out of energy by then, many global, regional, and local problems are connected with rising energy use. Global warming, for one, will be one of the big worries of the decades to come (we'll get back to this in Part Two). But there will also be many regional and local stresses. China will need one new 1,000-megawatt power plant every month. If all those new plants are based on coal, and with India also needing to expand power supplies at a considerable rate, acid rain could build up to a sizeable problem in Asia by 2020. For instance, acid rain could have a dramatic impact on Japan and its forests, just as it badly damaged spruce trees in the Adirondacks and red maples in Pennsylvania over the last decades.

In Nepal and other poor areas in the Himalayas, increasing fuelwood collection under pressure from rural population growth has contributed to the near-irreversible disappearance of the forest cover—with many negative consequences, including flooding in low-lying areas such as Bangladesh. And with a mix of deforestation and drought, people in some parts of Africa, such as Mauritania, see the desert advance 10 kilometers a year.

The list of stresses that will come with the population increase goes on—*infectious diseases, loss of tropical forests, fisheries depletion, biodiversity losses, pollution of the seas,* and *increasing water scarcity*, to name a few. Like global warming, these problems are all urgent global issues.

One more stress factor will accompany the surge in the sheer number of people: the *aging* of the world's population. It's already evident in many rich countries—by 2020, people over sixty will compose a third of the population in countries like Japan, Italy, and Spain, while Germany will be headed towards having more than two retirees for every three workers. But aging of the population also affects countries like China, where birth rates have been low for years. Expect enormous pressure on government budgets as, in country after country, pension payments soar in relation to the tax base. Also expect new immigration policies: Spain's and Germany's populations, for example, will shrink by more than 10–15 percent over the next four decades, requiring either more labor force participation (more people working and more working longer) or, more likely, massive inbound migration to stave off economic decline.

Still, outbound *migration* pressures in poor countries could dwarf the rich countries' need for inbound migration. Today's planet is so imbalanced that 20 percent of the world's people, those living in the thirty or so rich countries, consume 85 percent of the goods and services. Already close to 3 billion people, half the earth's inhabitants, live on less than $2 a day, with some 1.2 billion living in extreme poverty on less than $1 a day. In Africa, several hundreds of millions live on less than 60 cents a day. With 2 billion more coming, almost all in developing countries, the urge to migrate from poor countries to rich countries will become very pressing. Unless this imbalance is tackled in a major way, today's boat people and migrant smugglers may just be the harbingers of a great, poverty-induced pressure to vote with one's feet.

We'll return to this topic of *poverty* in Part Two as well. I could go on and on giving examples of the negatives the demographic force will bring—in fact it brings nothing but stresses.[5] Not so for the second force, which brings both unprecedented positives and negatives.

3
Doing Everything Differently: The New World Economy and the Two Revolutions Behind It

The other big force bringing spectacular changes to this planet over the next twenty years is the "new world economy," a broader and more interesting concept than the Internet-centered "new economy" we hear so much about. The difference will become clear as you read on.

This new world economy has two engines behind it (see Figure 1.1). The first is a kind of technological revolution, the second a kind of economic revolution. Let's start with the second one.

Economic Revolution

The economic revolution is easy to summarize: in the past twenty years, we went from 1.5 billion people living in market economies to nearly 6 billion. There are virtually no countries that haven't adopted market-oriented policies by now. Most have lowered their trade barriers, privatized public enterprises when it makes sense, made the state less a business operator and more a regulator and challenger, and opened public utilities to competition. More generally, they have given markets an increasing say and limited the role of civil servants.[1] Even the handful of exceptions, including Cuba and North Korea, are vaguely beginning to prepare for a transition.

The main reason: with the collapse of communism, everyone seems to have concluded that the alternative to the market—armies of highly imperfect bureaucrats trying to run a highly imperfect central planning system through millions of highly imperfect instructions—is gone for good. Besides bringing down Russia's gross domestic product (GDP) to the level of the Netherlands' today, this system left us little but a few juicy anecdotes, such as the time the USSR sent snowplows to Guinea.

Because this revolution is based more on hard-won experience than ideology, it goes very deep: despite Asia's financial crisis in 1997–1998, no developing country has moved back to a nonmarket model. And it's no longer a matter of right or left on the political spectrum: in Nepal a few years ago, I was able to have a good technical conversation about the pros and cons of privatization with a Marxist-Leninist minister, one of the last of his breed. On July 1, 2001, China's President Jiang Zemin decided to allow capitalist entrepreneurs to join the Communist Party.[2]

The only real debate today is about how to balance the basic market-oriented approach with this or that regulatory feature or social safety policy. But while this important debate is going on (most vividly in Europe, but not just there), no one in his right mind seriously contemplates any sort of wholesale return to central planning or even to state enterprise. This is all the more remarkable as most societies, perhaps even most people, harbor deeply some ambiguous feelings about the world of corporations and profit seeking.[3]

Whether we like it or not, the economic revolution is here to stay. Deep down, it is one of the two engines behind the new world economy. Even the events of September 11, which have led to a reassertion of the state in security-related matters, haven't throttled down that engine—to the contrary, see the fresh resolve with which nations went to the November 2001 Doha meeting of the World Trade Organization (WTO) and launched a new trade round.

Technological Revolution

The other engine behind the new world economy, the technological revolution, may be even more powerful. The two may actually be linked—the demise of central planning is often dated to the Soviet leadership's realization, in the 1980s, that a few U.S.-made fighter jets loaded with electronics could defeat an entire swarm of MIGs.

This technological revolution is centered on low-cost telecommunications and information technologies, which have spurred all kinds of side revolutions—in advanced materials, nanotechnology (very small things), robots mimicking or outdoing humans, biotechnology, and much else. And smart electronics now cover every conceivable aspect of human activity: of the billions and billions of chips embedded everywhere, those outside computers vastly outnumber those within.

Even old sectors like transportation have been revolutionized through the use of containers, tracking systems, hub airports, overnight shipping, and so forth—all made possible by the new communications and computer technologies. The fundamental point about these technologies is that they are *completely* changing the way things are done in business, in society, and everywhere. Why?

Simply put, earlier technological revolutions had to do with transforming energy or transforming materials. This one has to do with the transformation of time and distance, and thus cuts deeply into the fabric of society. At least as important, it has made knowledge and creativity the number one factor of production—far more important than capital, labor, and raw materials.

A second way of looking at the magnitude of this revolution: when we domesticated steam in the late 1700s and early 1800s, we went from one horse to 1,000 horsepower engines. The step-up was 10 to the power of 3. By comparison, the recent step-up in telecommunication bandwidth has been 10 to the power of 4, and in computers, a stunning 10 to the power of 5.

Here's a third perspective. In the 1800s, production processes had to be crammed into a small factory space because all the machines had to be connected to the single shaft of a steam engine. The spread of electricity in the early 1900s enabled small electrical motors to power each production step individually. The wire brought freedom from the shaft—and caused the great soaring in the size of factory floors and the ever-finer industrial division of labor.

As we enter the twenty-first century, we're back to some sort of shaft concept: the new communication possibilities create *virtual* information shafts that span the world—and to which production processes can be flexibly attached, from anywhere and at any time.

As these two revolutions—the economic and the technological—join forces, they power a new world economy intensely different from the one before. Don't get sidetracked by those who say that the dot-com implosion of 2000 and 2001 means that we have never left the old economy. They are about as farseeing as the ones who mistook the boom and bust of railway stocks in the 1840–1845 period for the end of industrialization—or those who would have concluded, from the collapse of most of the 3,000 automobile start-ups between 1900 and 1925, that the car industry would not go very far. They confuse the limited, high-tech-focused "new economy" with the much broader and deeper phenomenon that (precisely to mark the difference) I have labeled the "new world economy." Because it has not one but two engines behind it, the new world economy goes well beyond the mere use of new technologies: it's about new markets, new products, new ways of doing things—in short, a new mindset, as we will see in the next chapter.

You Ain't Seen Nothing Yet

The technological revolution still has a long life ahead of it. Moore's famous law, according to which engineers double the processing power of a computer chip every eighteen months, is still ticking along—and will lead to further rapid decreases in computing costs. By 2010, a typical computer will have more than 10 million times the power of a 1975 computer, at a much lower cost.[4] What's more, global computer grids are being worked on to provide computing power on tap, several million times more powerful than the Internet—IBM is reportedly a major investor in this. The heart of these grids will be programs that make collaborative computing and searches much easier and more reliable than they are today.

Even communications technology will continue leaping ahead, in both affordability and reach. The World Bank forecasts further major declines in telecommunications costs, to maybe 3 cents an hour for a transatlantic telephone call well before 2020—close to free. In Chile, a savvy privatization scheme—in which among other things, bidders for regional licenses must agree to cover remote areas, the winner being the one using the least subsidy to achieve this—has both produced a large increase in the number of lines and extended coverage to isolated areas. In China, the telecommunications market is soaring at rates exceeding 20 percent a year: by 2005, there could be 500 million lines, with 60 percent of them mobile, and some 200 million Internet users.[5] More broadly, cellular phones are spreading like wildfire throughout the developing world.[6] Amazingly, at the end of 2001, there were more mobile lines in Africa than fixed lines.[7]

These unstoppable developments promise even more spectacular leaps in the *density* of communications among businesses, people, and locations. If anything, the new world economy may be just beginning—some believe that it still has 80 percent of the way to go, with the world maybe halfway up the curve for computers, but still in the early takeoff stages for the Internet and related technologies. Others point to a powerful triplet just at its beginnings—information and communications technologies; biotechnologies and neuroscience; and renewable energy technologies.[8]

It's important to get a sense of how different this new world economy is before we move to the opportunities and stresses it produces. But there is another reason for digging further into this, even though this book is not about the new world economy itself: the mechanisms at its heart may just be those that can lead us on to new shapes for human institutions and new approaches to global problem-solving. Some people have aptly called the new world economy a "networked economy," and in Part Three we'll explore a twin, which one could call "networked governance."

4
Why the New World Economy Is So Radically Different

There's nothing like a few examples to get a sense of how profoundly different the new world economy is. Here are five among many.

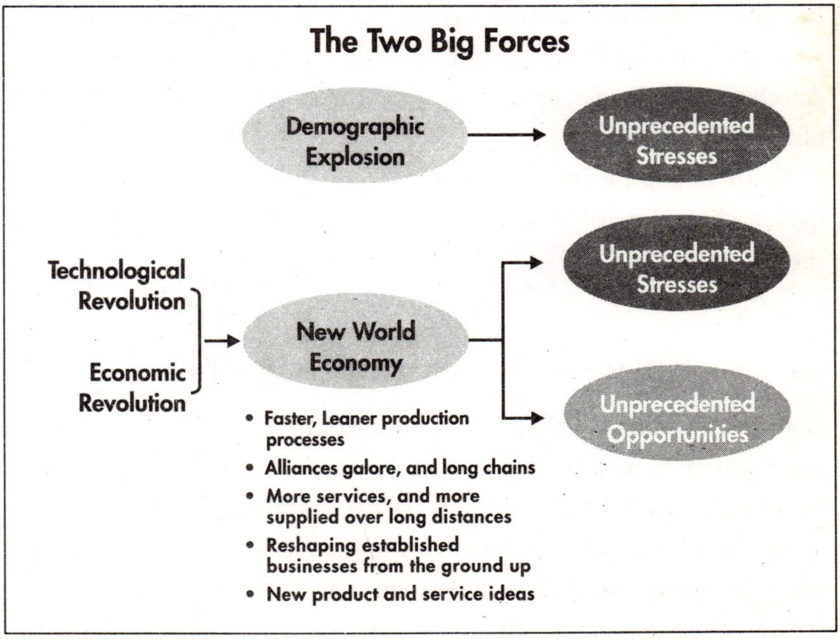

FIGURE 4.1 *The New World Economy*

Faster, Leaner Production Processes

Faster, leaner, just-in-time production processes are spreading everywhere. Toyota and Ford save billions of dollars by basing all their operations on this principle. Singapore runs its entire economy on this basis—the time to clear a shipload of goods through customs is down to less than half an hour. In Morocco, workers assemble pants whose parts have just been cut by a machine remotely controlled by a Netherlands-based computer, instantaneously reflecting the demand in the Dutch client's stores. In the United States, the ratio of inventories to sales in durable goods was cut by half between 1990 and 2000. These days, you don't keep inventories—you keep on your toes.

From its base in the disadvantaged province of Galicia, the very successful Spanish retailer Zara operates in such a stripped-down, real-time manner that it can make an entirely new clothing line from start to finish in three weeks, against an industry average of nine months.[1] In Hong Kong, manufacturers now produce an electric motor, say, for a hair dryer, less than six weeks after getting the specifications—working with the faraway client through computer-assisted design systems. Another example of agility: American Airlines reportedly makes 40,000 tariff changes a day.

So there is a pickup in speed—shorter design cycles, production cycles, shorter marketing loops, shorter pricing cycles. It's an age for the fast and lean.

Alliances Galore, and Long Chains

Consider a second example of how different this new world economy is: the number of mergers between companies has exploded (peaking in volume at more than $3 trillion in 1999), and there are ten times more alliances between companies than there were in 1990—even despite occasional reversals, such as those today in telecommunications.

More than the mergers, it's the new forms of alliances that are particularly telling. These now go well beyond the traditional joint venture model to include all kinds of joint production agreements, marketing agreements, research linkups, sharing of facilities, and swaps. A big pharmaceutical firm hooks up with a small biotech firm, a computer giant with software startups. Several universities get together around an international degree program. Airlines form alliances for joint flights and frequent-flier miles. In a recent amazing example, archrivals Suzuki and Kawasaki decided to team up in motorcycle design and parts purchases. Unlike mergers, these alliances are really partnerships—the partners keep their individual identities.

More broadly, partnership chains are getting longer. For instance, a Singapore manufacturer produces telephones in China for the U.S. market with Taiwanese capital and an Israeli technology license—five countries in the chain. Africa, too, is getting more involved: some garment manufacturers based in Hong Kong supply U.S. firms like DKNY from factories in Lesotho.[2] Remember the image of worldwide, virtual information shafts to which businesses can attach from anywhere. It's an age for those who are good at networking.

More Services, and More Supplied over Long Distances

Services capture an increasing share of countries' GDP: already above 80 percent in the United States, about 65 percent and rising in Europe. Manufacturing employment in America started at 20 percent of total employment in the early 1900s, went up to 35 percent in the 1950s, and is back down below 20 percent now.[3] New ideas for services spring up all the time in advanced countries, making the service sector the most vibrant, resilient, and job-creating part of the economy. Services are at the heart of the new world economy.

But there's an even newer phenomenon: services that were not traded at all some ten years ago are now routinely traded over long distances. Some 30,000 people in the Caribbean are manning call centers on behalf of U.S. businesses. Insurance companies in the United States fly their paperwork overnight to Ireland, where workers living in small villages log it into the companies' computers. The U.S. insurer Aetna even employs 400 people that way in Accra, Ghana.[4]

India's Bangalore now exports $7–8 billion in software services a year, from near zero a mere ten years ago. In Washington, DC, doctors dictate memos into a telephone and have them back within hours, typed by satellite-connected trained nurses in India. These long-distance services may open the way for up to $250 billion a year of new exports by the developing countries—a huge potential for them.

Reshaping Established Businesses from the Ground Up

In *Blown to Bits*, probably the most profound book about why so many things will be done differently from here on, Philip Evans and Tom Wurster put their finger at the heart of it all.[5] There used to be a tradeoff, they argue, between the reach of a message and its richness. A rich, detailed message required a one-on-one conversation; reaching out to thousands, for example, through advertising, meant you could send only simplistic messages. That tradeoff has now been killed by the new technologies: you can have rich, detailed, customized information flowing from one to thousands or millions. You can have your cake and eat it, too.

What does this do? Among other things, it reshapes businesses. Deep down, as economist Ronald Coase has shown, the boundaries of businesses (what gets done in-house and what's farmed out for others to do) are based on avoiding costs. The demise of the reach-richness tradeoff changes this cost equation—and thus changes everything:

- For example, companies can now outsource entire areas of their activity to subcontractors, and they do. This can even go to extremes: Cisco and Alcatel, two equipment makers, have decided to leave manufacturing to others altogether.[6]

- Companies can more readily enlist their customers and suppliers in the management of their affairs. Large firms like GE, IBM, and oil companies use the Internet to set up private or open business-to-business exchanges and marketplaces, through which they save up to 15 percent of their immense procurement budgets. Involving suppliers can go very far: in GM's Gravatai plant in Brazil, seventeen suppliers assemble modules that snap together into 100,000 Chevrolet subcompact cars a year. More and more companies involve suppliers in design and engineering, at savings of up to 40 percent.

- Armies of salespeople are becoming a thing of the past. Companies increasingly turn their customer relationships into a vivid market space with an unprecedented ability to customize products and services—making the customer *really* king.[7]

- In the years to come, you'll see a new breed emerge more and more: big "assemblers" of other companies' products and services, who will vastly simplify the lives of customers through their scouting and packaging work. Part of their role could be to protect customers' privacy from the tendency of on-line suppliers to secretly accumulate information about their visitors. Expect these assemblers, or "infomediaries" as some call them, to acquire great power over their suppliers, and, through their brands, over their attention-short customers.

New Product and Service Ideas

Far too much attention has gone to e-commerce conducted over the Internet, and to the implosion of those dot-coms that were riding on it. Still, despite recent setbacks—more marked in the business-to-customer end of e-commerce than in business-to-business applications—there is little doubt that Internet-based e-commerce will become a many-trillion-dollar phenomenon as we move towards 2020. This said, it's worth repeating once more how important it is to see the new world economy as a far broader phenomenon than the Internet-based economy. Consider three examples of how products and services evolve.

First, *products are becoming more like services*. Rather than buying a car, you are increasingly buying the service that goes with it. Leasing turns your capital outlay into a sort of rent. You can insure against defects and even wear and tear. Some manufacturers even pay for a hotel if your car breaks down, and soon some cars will even book themselves for service on their own. Time-sharing of corporate jets and even riding horses is soaring.[8] Customers of the U.S. company Andersen Windows can design a perfectly fitting, nonstandard window and get it delivered in short order by using a special software program made available by the firm. Is it a window, or is it a service? Products and services are getting blurred to the point where "the product is merely a service waiting to happen."[9]

Second, *giving things away* has become routine, because in the new world economy, where many things get turned upside down, it can make sense. Besides free e-mail, press, or information services on the Internet, examples are multiplying. In a stunning recent case, Michelin invented a revolutionary tire that will keep its shape even after being punctured and thus enable you to keep driving, even to a remote garage. What did Michelin do? Rather than hog this giant new market alone, it shared the technology with its competitors Pirelli and Goodyear—to create a new standard.[10] Similarly, Motorola, which files about 1,000 patents every year, recently decided to make its research available to outsiders, even potential competitors.[11] And by now, the free Linux operating system runs on more than 25 percent of high-end server computers, compared with 40 percent for Microsoft Windows.

Third, *bundling and unbundling* things in new ways is another hallmark of the new world economy. Airlines are now mere umbrella organizations for dozens of firms that own the airplanes, clean them up, run the bookings, handle the luggage, supply the catering, and so forth. Hollywood studios often assemble hundreds of firms around a movie. And one of the great changes ahead is in the banking industry, which, by 2020, could well have unbundled itself into three industries: creating financial products (more of an investment banking specialty), interfacing with customers (more of a traditional commercial banking specialty), and running the back office (the paperwork accompanying transactions, which even nonbankers can do anywhere in the world).[12]

An example of bundling to come: multi-use smart cards with biometric data that would serve simultaneously as identity cards; airport security devices; credit or debit cards; frequent flyer, hotel, and car rental cards; telephone cards; medical insurance cards; and even voter registration. Finland has already introduced a national identity card with some of these features, and Malaysia is experimenting.[13]

The new world economy is full of such radically different ways of doing things, many of which have nothing to do with the Internet and the narrow "new economy" concept that has become attached to it. It's more like *a new mindset*—brought about by the twin economic and technological revolutions that are behind all this.

5
The Opportunities and Stresses of the New World Economy

Have another look at our map in Figure 5.1 to see where we are going next. The new world economy, as the big second force of change for the next twenty years, brings both opportunities and stresses—unlike the demographic force, which has few redeeming features.

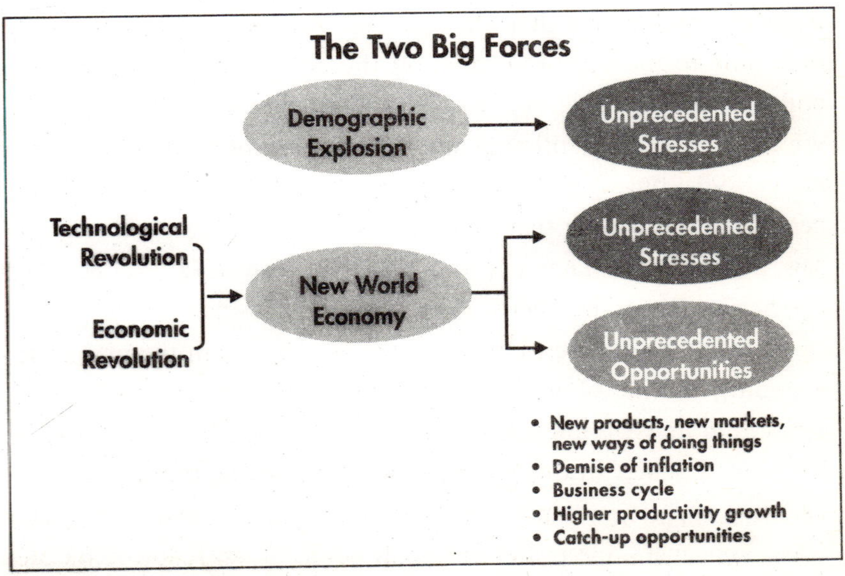

FIGURE 5.1 *The New World Economy—Unprecedented Opportunities*

Opportunities

Let's start with the opportunities. They come in five categories.

First, the new world economy brings, as the examples in Chapter 4 illustrate, *new products, new markets, and entirely new ways of doing things*.

Second, it also seems to spell the *demise of inflation* as we knew it. One cause was better monetary policy across the globe after New Zealand in 1990 bravely led the world's central banks to targeting inflation itself. But the main factor, and perhaps the main reason for the very success of that inflation targeting, may be the less inflation-prone environment created across the globe by the very fluid new world economy with its twin economic and technological revolutions.[1]

In the new world economy, price increases don't easily stick, as business has become hypercompetitive. Prices can be compared instantaneously across an increasingly transparent world—creating what some people have called half-jokingly the "nude economy." What's more, goods production and even services can relocate easily from one spot to another cheaper one. And financial markets are now able to monitor and sanction the economic policies of each country in real time. No wonder inflation rates have abated the world over—global inflation was 15–20 percent in the 1980s and early 1990s, but it fell below 10 percent by 1995 and below 5 percent by 2000. During that time span, the developing country group saw their inflation rates fall from 30–40 percent to a level equal to the rich countries' by 2000.

Third, the *business cycle* isn't what it used to be. In the new world economy, country after country will gradually increase the share of services in its GDP towards the 80 percent or so already achieved in the United States. In this context, the old recurring business cycle—excessive capacity and inventory buildups in the manufacturing sector (cars, appliances, electronic goods) in boom times, followed by production cutbacks to run inventories down again—becomes a more limited, less discernible phenomenon.

Even before being amplified by the September 11, 2001, terrorist attack, the 2000 U.S. slowdown and the ensuing 2001 recession were clearly different from this older cycle. It wasn't a cycle at all. Rather, it was more like a bad onetime hangover, or "tech correction," reflecting two things: stock market losses after an incredible overvaluation of technology stocks; and a brutal slowdown in high technology orders after an equally incredible orgy of such investments by businesses.[2] The steepness of the manufacturing sector's decline may actually have had something to do with the just-in-time methods described above, which increase the speed of transmission. What was also new was the speed with which slowdowns in the United States, Europe, Japan, and the emerging markets started to interact.

Even so, the large service sector has somehow acted like a flywheel well into 2001. Even if the jury is still out on this, it looks as if the old consumption- and manufacturing-led business cycle may become less of a recurring feature—if so, happily a victim of the new world economy.

Fourth, the new world economy seems to bring about *higher productivity growth.* After extensive recalculations in 1997 of the true level of inflation in the United States, economists got a first inkling that inflation had been overstated to the tune of one percentage point and that the annual rate of growth of productivity had for more than a decade been higher than believed.[3] Indeed, the very high growth rates of the U.S. economy in the second half of the 1990s seemed to confirm that something extraordinary was happening around productivity trends.

Although those figures have now been revised back downward, and despite a lingering debate among academics on this, the pickup in productivity growth seems clear. For the United States, for example, productivity growth has been 2.5 percent per year in 1995–2000, against about 1.5 percent in 1973–1995. And that gain is worth a lot: for the United States alone, a one-percentage point increase in productivity growth is worth $1 trillion in additional wealth over a decade. Even if a more sober reading cut the estimate to only one-half a percentage point, this would still be worth some

$400 billion. Interestingly, U.S. productivity growth has been holding up well even into the third and fourth quarters of 2001, despite the September 11 events.[4]

What's behind this? For starters, the new ways of doing things illustrated in Chapter 4. Probing deeper, Larry Summers, the former U.S. Treasury secretary, may have put his finger on the crux. In a speech given in May 2000, he observed that the new world economy seems to behave differently from the old industrial and agricultural age models. "Consider the classic cycle of wheat: when prices rise, farmers produce more, consumers buy less, and equilibrium is restored at a lower level of demand." This, he said, is a "negative-feedback economy," limited by short-term supply-and-demand constraints.

"By contrast, the new information economy will increasingly be a positive-feedback economy," he continued. In the old economy, things start out rare and expensive before they become widespread and cheaper: think of television sets, cars, washing machines. In the new world economy, additional capacity becomes available so quickly and inexpensively (think of cellular phones, microchips, new Internet services) that traditional supply constraints become almost unimportant. In effect, the economy's speed limit has been raised.[5]

But the story goes even beyond the impact of the new technologies. Studies by the U.S. Conference Board and by the McKinsey consultancy show how increasing flexibility in labor, capital, and product markets, as well as more effective forms of business organization, have also played a role in raising this speed limit—reminding us about the first engine behind the new world economy, the economic revolution.[6]

Fifth, besides these general, worldwide benefits, the new world economy brings unprecedented *catch-up opportunities* for the developing countries. Many of them could benefit disproportionately from the opportunities brought by new technologies and new ways of doing things. Remember Bangalore's software services exports, garment assembly in Lesotho, and U.S. insurance paperwork in Ghana. Here are a few more examples.

A few years ago, China started thinking about how to equip 400 million Chinese with smart cards enabling them to receive or make payments. If this were to happen, and nothing stands in the way, China would jump over generations of banking developments straight into the era of electronic money—saving itself a lot of trouble on the way. Lithuania and Poland are looking at similar leapfrogging.

In education, the opportunities are equally tremendous. To give just one example: in Mexico, the Monterrey Tech university has in a few years become one of the world's foremost distance learning systems, with some thirty connected campuses across Latin America offering each student access to the same star professor. In many developing countries, teacher networking over the Internet is leading to better curriculum development and rapid exchanges of best practices.

There are also some stunning village-level examples. In Côte d'Ivoire, farmers check cocoa prices directly on the Chicago commodities exchange through village cell phones—no longer depending on the biased price indications of local traders. In Ethiopia, a colleague of mine asked a rural audience who among them knew about the Internet, expecting to draw a blank. A farmer promptly replied that he used the Internet to sell goats to Ethiopian taxi drivers in New York eager to make a present to their families back home for traditional celebrations. By now, several specialized nongovernmental organizations help village women in Latin America and Asia post their handicraft products straight into a web catalog, together with their story and that of their villages.[7] From nowhere and almost overnight, all these people are suddenly part of the global market.

The new world economy is thus full of unprecedented, wonderful opportunities. But it also brings its load of stresses, which come under four categories—see Figure 5.2 on page 31.

Stresses

The first type of stress has to do with *adapting to the new rules of the game* of the new world economy. Several books have been written on these new rules.[8] Yet I find myself returning again and again to four basic features of the new world economy and to the four new rules that I believe they imply. Actually, you can readily deduce them from the examples provided in Chapters 3 and 4.

The new world economy has four features:

- It is *bent on speed*—so you have to be *agile*. Bill Gates calls it "velocity."

- It flows *across national boundaries*—so you must be plugged in and *good at networking* internationally.

- It is highly *knowledge-intensive*—so you must be good at constantly *learning*. If you stand still, you fall back.

- It is *hypercompetitive*—so you must be 100-percent *reliable*, or business will shift to someone else.

Whether they like it or not, countries, sectors, companies, organizations, and individuals alike must heed these new rules of the game—which increasingly define success and failure. The distinction between rich and poor is now accompanied by other stark distinctions: between fast and slow; good at networking and not plugged-in; constantly learning and being static. And between entirely reliable and anything less. As all players adjust to these new rules, expect a lot of stress—the unpleasant kind that comes with having to change habits and learn new tricks under outside pressure, even as you thought you were doing fine.

The second type of stress relates to the previous one, and has to do with *growing disparities*—between countries and within them. As we just saw, the new world economy is good to those who are fast, good networkers, good learners, and highly reliable. Indeed, it brings immense rewards to those who possess these features—some analysts even went overboard and talked about a "winner-take-all society."[9] At any rate, the new world economy badly marginalizes countries that lack these features, even as it rewards the more favored, thus leading to increasing disparities *between* countries.

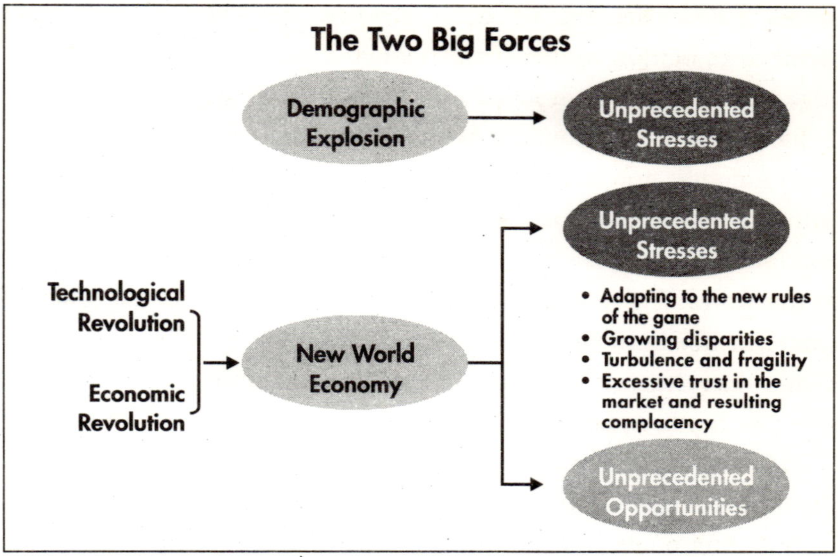

FIGURE 5.2 *The New World Economy—Unprecedented Stresses*

The ratio between the income of the twenty richest countries and that of the poorest countries has doubled to 40 to 1 over the last four decades. The new world economy could aggravate these disparities.[10] Among developing countries, the greatest concern is for a subgroup of about fifty so-called "least developed countries," mostly in Africa, which are in danger of missing out entirely within the new world economy. So unless something dramatic is done (see Part Two), disparities between countries could increase in an already highly unequal world. And expect disparities within the developing country group to become larger as well: just think of Africa, with the growing contrast between Mauritius and the sub-Saharan African states, or of the diverging worlds of the Dominican Republic and Haiti sharing the same island.

There are also signs of mounting disparities *within* countries. In the United States, the ratio between the income of the top one-fifth of the population and that of the bottom one-fifth jumped from 18:1 in 1990 to 24:1 in 2000.[11] The compensation premium paid to a college graduate compared with a high-school graduate doubled over the same decade. This phenomenon, noticeable at first mostly across the Anglo-Saxon world, is now spreading to other countries: the new world economy seems to be bidding up the compensation of those who possess knowledge relative to that of unskilled workers.

Increasing within-country inequalities, visible since the 1980s in Latin America, now manifest themselves even in countries like China, with growing urban-rural gaps. Countries like Russia, the Kyrgyz Republic, and Armenia have rapidly become some of the most unequal in the world. These wider within-country disparities go beyond income: in northern Brazil, child mortality rates are now five times higher than those in the southern part of the country. Expect a lot of stress as they become more widespread.

The third category of stresses has to do with greater *turbulence and fragility* in the new world economy. There are all kinds of inklings of this.

Recurring bouts of financial market *turbulence*, of the sort seen in 1997–1998 in Asia, Russia, and Brazil, as well as more recently in Turkey and Argentina, could well be in store as the new world economy develops. Why? Consider two facts. First, the world's pool of stocks and bonds, only $10 trillion in 1980 and $30 trillion in 1990, is now above $80 trillion.[12] Second, an ever-increasing chunk of the financial markets is now in the hands of portfolio managers who are quicker than their predecessors at moving away from any suspect company, country, or region. It's as if the waves on the sea were becoming larger and more easily prone to suddenly change direction. This may actually have been the largest part of the story behind the Asian crisis of 1997–1998—even though crony capitalism, recklessly managed financial institutions, and unrealistic exchange rate policies clearly played their own nasty roles as well. At any rate, when the waves become larger and less predictable, even a well-managed smaller economy can capsize.

An additional source of turbulence is from the rapid pickup in the pace of change in the new world economy itself, beyond financial markets. Enterprises increasingly need to make enormous investment decisions in a context where their industries and business concepts are changing almost month to month. The result can be mega-mistakes that create major ripples. Example: telecommunications firms paid over $100 billion over the last few years for European 3G licenses, which would enable the Internet to come to cellular phones. But recent surveys show that only 4 percent of cellular customers may be really interested in this. It is still not clear what this haste will do to the firms and their banks.

Along with more turbulence and the stresses that go with it, the new world economy also breeds a new kind of potentially stressful *fragility*. Central banks find it harder and harder to manage what they are supposed to manage—and their role has become more symbolic than they care to admit. In late 1998, the scary crisis around the New York–based Long-Term Capital Management hedge fund showed how complex, poorly known financial creatures could produce fragility where no one had expected any.

And as the world's payment, settlement, and depositary systems become more integrated worldwide—something we can expect—their increased efficiency may come at the cost of a greater exposure of the whole system to one critical breakdown. The September 11, 2001, terrorist attack on the United States made many people realize how the enormous sheath of wires under Lower Manhattan's financial district had turned it into the world's largest electronic marketplace. When those millions of phone lines went dead, markets came close to seizing up entirely.

Add to this fragility the broader one that comes from the expanding use of the Internet to effect orders, keep trains running, redirect power supplies, and so forth. It would not be impossible for a few malicious people to knock off some key switching and addressing centers at the heart of the Internet. Until recently, one-fourth of Internet traffic apparently ran through one building in Tyson's Corner, Virginia—next to a local steakhouse. The U.S. government is now reportedly considering the creation of a secure government network independent of the Internet to make critical federal activities less vulnerable to cyber-attacks.[13]

Another example of fragility: the hub-and-spoke network developed by the U.S. airline industry since deregulation means that 80 percent of U.S. airline travel now takes off or lands at the busiest 1 percent of airports. If a problem hits one or a few big hubs, it ripples throughout the network. Expect to find more and more fragilities of this kind in the new world economy.

The fourth type of stress associated with the new world economy is subtler. It has to do with *excessive trust in the market, and the complacency that results from it.*

With the central planning model gone for good, more politicians and other players see the market as the solution to all problems, sometimes dumping on government while they are at it. Whether from intellectual laziness or from single-minded pursuit of ideology, what these free-market fundamentalists fail to see is that while central planners were either cretins or fools, the market is a moron. An effective moron, but a moron nevertheless: left to its own devices, it will churn away mindlessly.[14] There are two serious dangers in this complacency.

First, if we leave all problem-solving to the market, emerging social problems will be left unattended. For example, the new world economy seems to be making job tenures more precarious, even where unemployment remains low, as in the United States and some other countries. One answer to the feeling of insecurity this brings would be to make pensions more portable—but the market won't do this alone. And as we saw, the new world economy bids down the compensation terms of the unskilled relative to the skilled, in a short amount of time. Here again, one answer is to make sure that minimum wages do not end up ridiculously out of date, as they are in some rich countries. Again, the market alone won't do this. If we trust the market to solve all our problems, we'll end up with scores of unnecessary social stresses over the next twenty years—and a lot of protesters in the street.

There's a second, even more profound problem with trusting the market to find solutions to everything. The market's own mindless expansion, effective as it is in the short term, inevitably brings its own long-term problems as it further taxes the planet's carrying capacity beyond the already bad overload coming from the population increase. It's not a question of ideology, but of physical limits. A dying Japanese Zen master told his disciples: "I have learned only one thing in life: how much is enough."

About limits, the new world economy has no clue—nor do most politicians and thinkers, trained by the prosperous second part of the twentieth century to be overly market-trusting. Here lies a huge source of twenty-first century discussion or even dissent. The great economist John Maynard Keynes sensed this more than half a century ago when he wrote that the basic debate over the future of human society would eventually gyrate around just that—how much leeway to give to "the money-making and money-loving instincts as the main motive force of the economic machine."[15] Expect a lot of stress around this debate, and even more stress if it isn't resolved.

6
A Crisis of Complexity?

As we saw in the preceding chapters, the new world economy brings unprecedented opportunities to all kinds of players, including catch-up opportunities for developing countries able to seize them. But it also brings several categories of stresses—which add themselves to the long list of social and environmental stresses that accompany the population increase.

Like two geysers, the two forces of the population increase and the new world economy spew unprecedented complexity in economic, social, political, and environmental matters. Human problems are

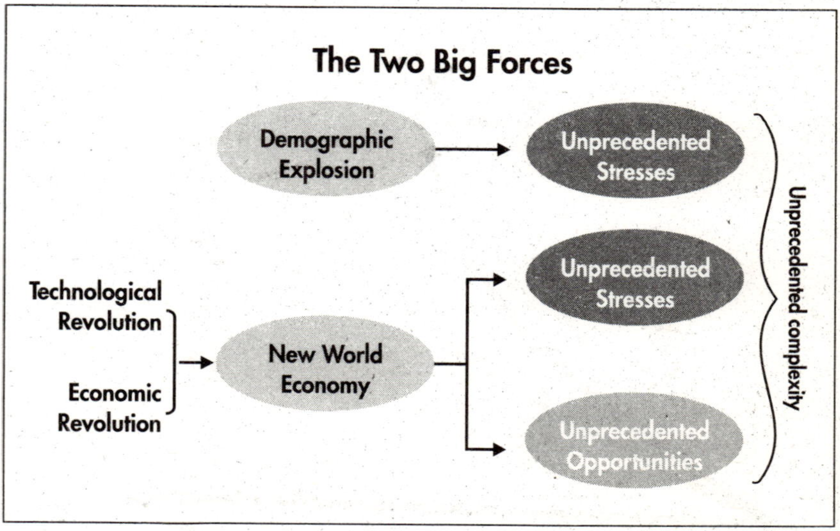

FIGURE 6.1 *The Two Big Forces—Unprecedented Complexity*

becoming more pressing, more global, and more difficult to solve—technically and politically. A crisis of complexity is brewing.

The rate of change produced by the two forces contrasts starkly with the slow evolution of human institutions. Whether they are nation-states, government departments, international organizations, or large outfits of any type, human institutions tend to evolve only slowly, in a linear way.

By contrast, the two forces of change are markedly exponential. The demographic force brings an *exponentiality of scarcity:* scarcer space, water, soil, clean air, animal and plant species, and so on.

Propelling the new world economy force is an *exponentiality of plenitude.* Remember Moore's law, Larry Summers's positive-feedback concept, and Evans and Wurster's point about killing the trade-off between reach and richness of messages (Chapters 4 and 5). Add in Metcalfe's law, which says that the value of a network increases with the square of its members. And recall some of the examples of new markets, new products, and new ways of doing things—for instance, how giving away products suddenly makes sense.

As the two exponential forces gain momentum, their curves move away from the linear change curve of human institutions. I like to represent this crudely this way:

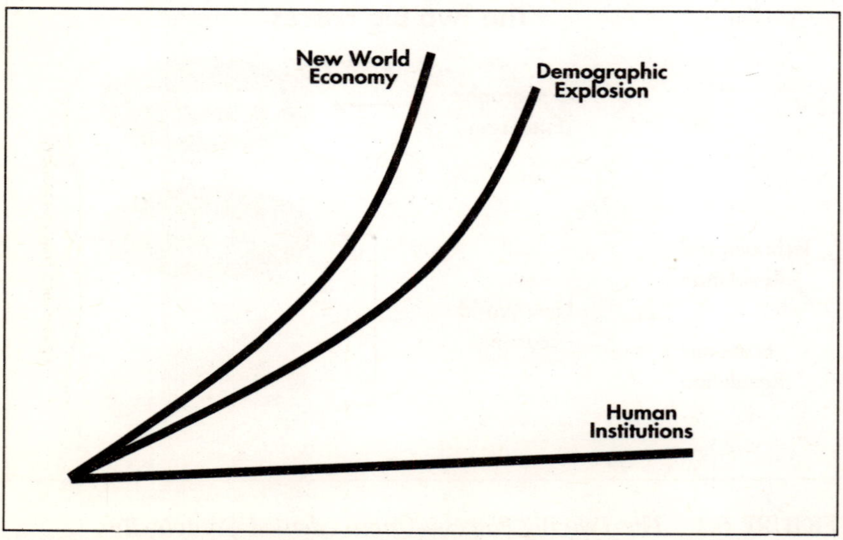

FIGURE 6.2 *The Two Big Forces—Graph*

What's more, time itself fractures into different fields. It flows in "dog years" along the demographic and new world economy curves. When a dog is two years old, we multiply by seven and say that it's fourteen years old in human terms. Along the demographic line, one year lost in the fight against global warming is like seven years lost, in a manner of speaking. Along the new world economy line, Amazon.com was worth some $15 billion three years into its existence—as if it had been around twenty-one years or so. Nokia, which not long ago used to produce toilet paper and other unglamorous products, has managed to build up a 35-percent share of the world market for cellular phones in a few years.[1]

By comparison, time flows in "bureaucratic years" along the human institutions line. Something one should be perfectly able to change in one year's time takes seven years to change. And so we have—if you allow me this quirky image—a great clash between dog years and bureaucratic years. No wonder people sense that two different clocks are ticking.

Let's have a closer look at the human institutions line—which itself will be massively under stress, as human institutions struggle to change.

7
Three New Realities

The main reason human institutions of all kinds are struggling to meet the momentous changes afoot is that they weren't designed for these changes. Particularly visible in those that are in charge of public governance, this struggle reaches beyond them and is defined by three new realities.

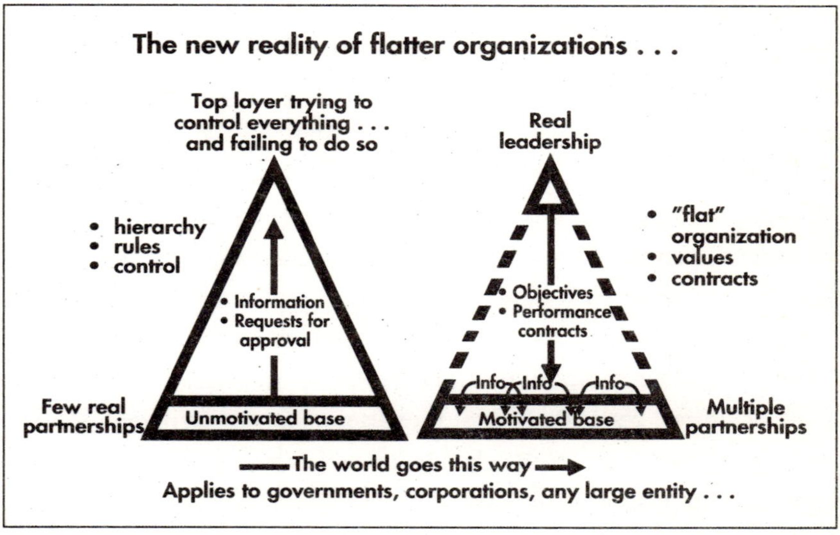

FIGURE 7.1 *The New Reality of Flatter Organizations*

From Hierarchy to Network

The first new reality has to do with the limitations of our inherited hierarchies and the need to move to nimbler forms of organization. Human institutions of all kinds—nations, governments, government units or agencies, multilateral institutions, churches, multinational companies, large outfits of any kind—tend to reflect a hierarchical organizational model inherited from the industrial age, even in a way from the agricultural age. In periods of intense and complex change, traditional hierarchies fall short—the future belongs to flatter, faster, more network-like organizations.

Why? In traditional hierarchies—the pyramid depicted on the left side of Figure 7.1—information gets piped up, through various middle and senior management layers, eventually reaching the leaders at the top. The system runs on layers, rules, and controls. But three bad things result when hierarchies find themselves surrounded with changes.

First, they lack flexibility and are slow to adapt to external changes. Information has a long way to go before it reaches the top. Each layer has some sort of vested interest in staying as it is; each is reluctant to pass on bad news up to the next level. The rules and controls, designed to do their job in stable times, also build in rigidity. When change intensifies, these things become liabilities.

Second, people in such organizations are used more as information transmitters than as independent agents. This hurts most when it comes to the morale and motivation of those who work in these hierarchies. Large hierarchies almost always harbor covertly or openly unhappy cultures, particularly at headquarters. Most of them end up with an unmotivated base. When change intensifies, many workers lack the motivation to respond quickly and in unaccustomed ways.

Third, and perhaps most important, the leaders at the top, who are supposed to control everything and call the shots, end up swamped when the rate of change is high. Those who manage international institutions wrestle with a daily stack of memos and reports one to two feet high, along with several hundred e-mails. In August 1997 in Thailand, at the onset of the Asian crisis, it was almost impossible to find able interlocutors among the leadership of the central bank and the government:

they were completely overwhelmed, and looking for the exits.

More generally, running major companies, government operations, civil society organizations—any large hierarchy—has become a panicky affair. Corporate chief executives last a shorter and shorter time on average, and honeymoon periods end fast.[1] Lately, a growing number of chief executives have abruptly abandoned the top rungs of the business ladder and opted for a new life—the heads of Carlsberg, AOL Time Warner, Energis, and Lazard London come to mind.

Hierarchies are thus not of the age we are entering. That does not mean all hierarchies are meant to die—there are many areas or functions that cannot do without them. But as a general model of human organizations, they are doomed—and largely responsible for the lagging behind of the human institutions line depicted in Figure 6.2. Hierarchies are just too slow, too rigid, too self-obsessed, too mired in a sort of perpetual bad mood. And most of the time, their leaders are in over their heads.

Expect the pressure of change to push towards new forms of organization—along the lines of the right-hand side of Figure 7.1. The new generation of organizations will be much more inspired by the concept of networks than by that of a pyramid-shaped hierarchy. They will be flatter, leaner, more flexible—without the many middle- and senior-management layers of traditional hierarchies.

Why? Because information won't be piped up all the way to the top. It will stay at the level of the organization's base—at the line level, where people connect to customers, suppliers, or partners. Information will stay at the level where it can readily be used to adapt to changing needs. And you'll see many partnerships blooming at that level—a concept that traditional hierarchies engage in less easily.

In those flatter, more network-like organizations, people won't be merely information transmitters—they will be empowered assets, acting independently. Yet leaders will retain an important role: not through controls and detailed instructions but by instilling the basic vision, values, and objectives into the organization and by holding employees to performance contracts. Leaders will exercise *real* leadership, in other words. As a result, such organizations will have a far more motivated base.

Pipe dream? No, reality in the making. Watch how one large corporation after another struggles to move from the left-hand triangle to the right-hand one. The equipment maker ABB and the NUCOR mini-mill company were early experimenters in the early 1990s—by now, most corporations have tried to move to the right. There's a whole industry of "change management" books on this theme. Churches, unions, universities—virtually all organizations of some size—are under pressure to change in the same direction. In the United States, there have even been proposals for a flattened military command structure, with more responsibility devolved to lower-level commanders, and smaller, more mobile forces operating over a large area—networked through information technology.

There are good reasons for this: flatter, more network-like organizations promise to be smarter and more adaptable, faster at turning themselves around than traditional hierarchies. When the rate of change picks up along with complexity, that's what is needed. Welcome to the new reality of information-age organizations—deeply different from the agricultural-age and industrial-age organizations of old.

Interestingly, in some ways it's forward, in some others it's backward. Behavioral scientists who have studied behavior in the new, flatter organizational environment remark that people behave much more like the hunter-gatherers of 20,000 years ago—forming temporary teams, remaining nimble, working long hours around a project and then taking breaks, and accepting only the sort of leadership that proves its worth.[2]

One sure thing: there will be a lot of stress as traditional organizations struggle to shift to the right-hand side. The struggle will be the greatest in public sector institutions, where rituals are deeply established; some of the world's most ritualistic organizations are ministries of foreign affairs, for example. Arguably, the country that has tried the hardest is New Zealand, where in the 1990s government was made to look much more like the right-hand side triangle than the left-hand one: top civil servants were given a balance sheet for their departments and extensive freedom to act, but had to meet goals set by the legislature or lose their position.

Expect many others to try similar things, despite the difficulties and controversies this entails.[3] More broadly, the move from hierarchies towards nimbler, more network-like organizations is clearly one of the

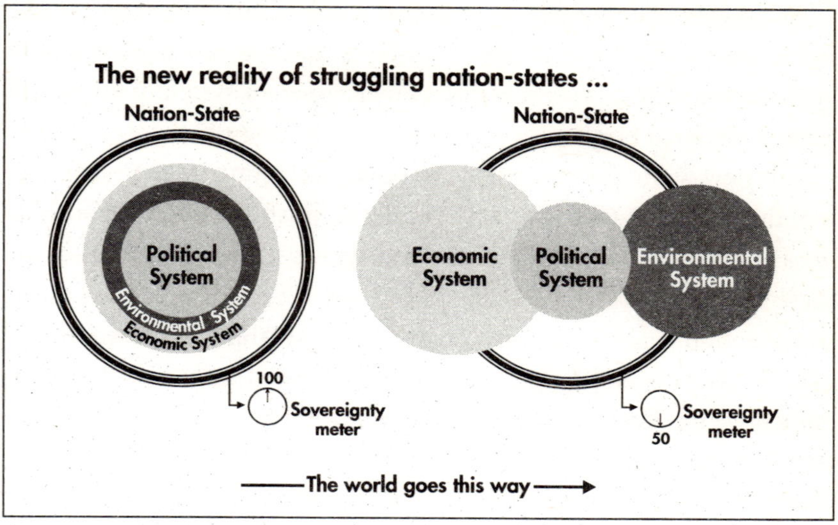

FIGURE 7.2 *The New Reality of Struggling Nation-States*

key ways to bring the human institutions line up—using the parlance of Figure 6.2.

The Struggling Nation-State

A second, equally stressful new reality has to do with the struggle of a trusted contraption—the nation-state. The nation-state and the concept of national sovereignty are not that old. Historians often date them back to the Peace of Augsburg in 1555, which said that each ruler decides his country's religion *(cuius regio, eius religio)*. More often, they are associated with the Treaty of Westphalia of 1648—when the powers of continental Europe wound up the Thirty Years War with the pledge to let each country be ruled as its ruler desired. The nation-state, which has kept evolving, is a territorial concept defined by a geographical border—the outer circle in Figure 7.2.

This simplified depiction says that inside that physical territory, you'll find a political system, an environmental system, and an economic system. When the nation-state is firmly in control of all three, the sovereignty meter is at 100—a figure of speech, because this condition has probably never existed.

What is happening now—and what will be happening more in the twenty years of intense change ahead—is that the two big forces will yank the economic system and the environmental system increasingly outside national borders.

The new world economy force, for one, is creating an economic system that straddles these borders. Recall the Washington doctors dictating their memos to satellite-connected typists in India. The profit for these transactions (which is significant—at 9 cents a line, the cost of transcription is about half that charged by a Washington-based typist) can be booked and taxed either in the United States or in India. Somehow, the United States is losing control, and so is India. The circle representing the economic system starts moving out of the territory. There are many other examples of this happening in Chapters 4 and 5 (and later in Chapter 14).

Similarly, the demographic force, with its various stresses, will yank the environmental system increasingly outside the border. Remember the Chinese coal-based power plants sending acid rain to Japan. Global warming, regional water shortages, and other stresses accompanying the population increase also dilute the nation-state's mastery over its environmental system. So do AIDS and drug-resistant tuberculosis, diseases that respect no boundaries and sweep through the world at a faster rate than before.

As this happens, the political system, delinked from the other two systems, ends up weakened. The sovereignty meter falls to 50—again, as a figure of speech.[4]

This phenomenon of the struggling nation-state does not come alone. It is accompanied by a growing sense of malaise about traditional politicians and politics. Everywhere, the world of traditional politics is being shaken up: voters are more prone to skip between political parties, and honeymoon periods are shorter and shorter. Surveys of young people in the United States and in Europe show a great disaffection for the traditional political class.[5]

Moreover, debates between the left and the right have given way to another form of debate: between those who resist the changes afoot and those who see them as opportunities. You'll find elements from both the political right and the left united in resisting changes and in seeing plots behind them.[6] Those who see opportunity in change—only 30 percent or so of the population, according to surveys done in America—often find those coalitions baffling.

The second new reality is thus a mixture: a struggling nation-state and mounting challenges to traditional politics together produce a sort of perpetual bad mood in political life. These days, newspapers abound with examples of this at the local, national, or global levels. The struggle of the nation-state itself is less visible. But make no mistake, it's a great historical struggle.[7]

A New Kind of Partnership

The third new reality has to do with how the public sector, business, and civil society interact. We're used to a mode of interaction where each party stays in its respective corner and there is little collaboration among them. In this mode, business does its own thing and concentrates only on the bottom line, encouraged to do so by theoreticians like Milton Friedman. Civil society keeps to its role of criticizing from the outside, rarely doing the more courageous bit of offering practical solutions to public scrutiny. And government arrogantly believes in its

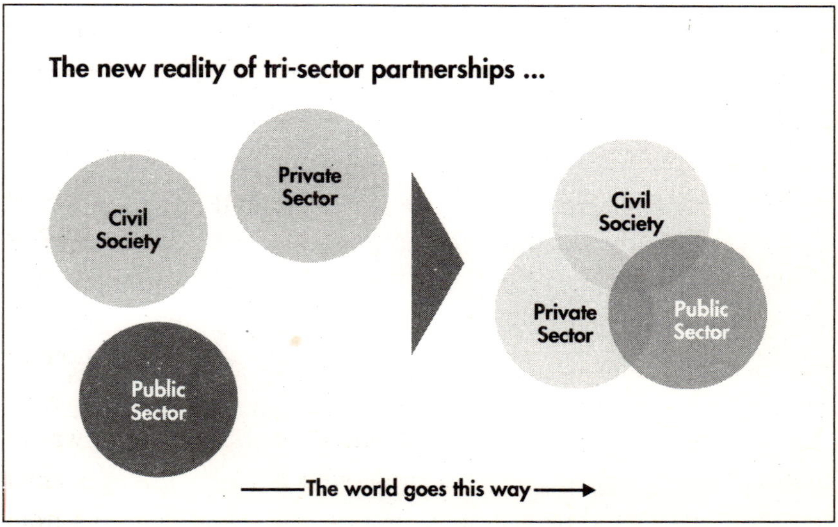

FIGURE 7.3 *The New Reality of Tri-Sector Partnerships*

ability to know what needs fixing, what's good for you, how things should be handled.

As change becomes faster and deeper, this separation is no longer tenable. Why?

First, *civil society*—nongovernmental organizations (NGOs), advocacy groups, unions, religious organizations—has become a powerful force. The number of known international NGOs went from 6,000 in 1990 to 26,000 in 2000. Within countries, NGOs and other elements of civil society are also a major force: the United States has some 2 million, with 70 percent of them created since the 1970s. Even in Eastern Europe, more than 100,000 NGOs have sprung up in a decade. And some are huge: the World Wide Fund for Nature has 5 million members.

Beyond sheer numbers, civil society has also become more powerful through its increasingly deft use of new technologies. Thousands of web sites, instant news services, and alert systems have sprung up and are being used to form powerful coalitions of NGOs and other civil society groups. Civil society excels at taking advantage of the death of the reach-richness trade-off (discussed in Chapter 4).

It is also in part thanks to these new technologies that an ever-growing fringe of civil society has even turned itself into a vigorous global protest alliance. A pillar of that alliance has been the electronic network of activists centered around Berkeley, Portland, and Seattle, but there are many others, as well as networks of networks. From Seattle to Genoa, these critics have united in large protest coalitions, largely glued together through Internet-based coordination: some have talked about "NGO swarms." In Washington in the spring of 2000, during meetings of the International Monetary Fund (IMF) and the World Bank that had attracted some 10,000 protesters, you had an amazing contrast: stranded finance ministers unable to cross picket lines or to find out where meetings had been relocated, and, on the other hand, protesters' web sites where you could watch the entrance of the IMF live, find out the current direction of the wind in case the police used tear gas, and see the detailed agendas and schedules of delegations.

But the increasing voice and importance of civil society has other causes than sheer numbers, a clever use of technology, and the ability to coalesce into protest alliances. Deep down, some groups in this sector are well ahead of the other two sectors in detecting the momentous changes to come, and are ahead in their global activism—and the public at large senses that. This is why civil society is on its way up in people's minds: surveys in the United States and Europe show the public at large trusting civil society far more than government, business, or even the media. This builds a raw but genuine form of legitimacy. Some people question that legitimacy, calling it nonrepresentative or even "the tyranny of the unelected." But once they've made that point, it's not clear what they mean to do about it.

Most important, some civil society institutions possess extensive knowledge in many fields—such as the environment, education, health, and even financial markets. It is hard to see how complex social, environmental, and economic problems can be solved without that knowledge—and without the special perspective that civil society institutions bring.

It is also hard to see how the complex problems of the next twenty years can be solved without the active engagement of *business*. Like civil society, large corporations have a huge advantage over governments—the advantage of being global. While nation-states struggle to maintain their territorial concept of sovereignty, large multinationals are spreading their operations across many countries—more than 100, for the largest among them.

Whether they are part of the problem or part of the solution, businesses possess an advantage in knowledge and sheer means. When an outfit like Cisco Systems decides to engage in the education field, it can leverage its effort across scores of countries at a time: by 2001, 157,000 students had enrolled in the 6,800 "networking academies" it had established in a short time in some 130 countries.[8] And when it comes to many of the urgent global issues detailed in Part Two, business will clearly be called on to contribute to their solutions as never before: with breakthroughs in renewable energy, desalination, new vaccines and drugs, safer banking, more sustainable forestry—you name it. Big business can even become a helpful global enforcer: for instance, Unilever has pledged that from 2005 on, it will only buy from fisheries that are certifiably sustainable; and California's giant private pension fund Calpers recently caused quite a stir when it decided to pull out from a number of countries that failed to meet its human rights, labor conditions, and financial transparency thresholds.

And businesses, particularly large multinational companies, do a better job than many governments of looking beyond the next few years. It was Shell, not governments, that pioneered the use of long-term scenarios to explore the future in richer ways than those afforded by traditional planning.[9] More generally, over the last two decades, it has been fascinating to watch quite a few large companies move through four stages of increasing "corporate responsibility." First, some had small charity departments. Then, as they were attacked by NGOs regarding labor practices and the environmental consequences of their activities, they created larger corporate responsibility departments. Next, some became agents of development of their own, like Cisco with its academies. Now some are seriously interested in participating with government and civil society in urgent problem-solving going far beyond their own fields—not for a direct commercial reason, but because, like civil society, they too are beginning to seriously wonder what state the world will be in ten or fifteen years from now.[10]

What has happened is that civil society and business have, in effect, begun to complement the effort of beleaguered *public sectors*. Why beleaguered? For one, because of the rising complexity of human affairs. Think of the federal regulators facing the 1998 collapse of the Long-Term Capital Management hedge fund, dumbfounded by the size and complexity of the positions they discovered.[11] Think of the even greater stupor in U.S. government circles at the sheer range and complexity of the problems that led to the December 2001 collapse of Enron, a huge, unregulated energy company that traded in some 2,000 products, from weather derivatives to bandwidth. Think of telecom regulators trying to regulate an industry that changes every six months. Think of municipal employees facing the massive urban congestion ten years from now in Asia.

Compounding all this is a worrisome trend: all over the world, the best and the brightest increasingly stay away from public service.[12] In

1980, three-fourths of the graduates of Harvard's Kennedy School of Government went to work for government; today only one-third do. In much of the world, government salaries at middle level are way below those of equivalent private-sector positions. It's even much worse at the higher level: Alan Greenspan, the head of the U.S. Federal Reserve, is paid a modest $140,000 a year, perhaps one-tenth of what a decently good government bond trader used to get in the late 1990s. No wonder that increasingly, very capable young civil servants see their public careers merely as launching pads: the French Treasury, for example, finds it harder and harder to hang on to its best staff.

For all these reasons, forget about government—federal, regional, local—being able to solve tomorrow's complex problems *alone*, without major help from the other two sectors of society. These problems are so ominous and challenging that the three sectors must combine their knowledge and their energy to get them solved.

All this leads to an important new reality: it will take partnerships among government, business, and civil society to solve intractable problems. Odd as they may feel at first—they require an entirely different attitude from what we are used to—expect such tri-sector partnerships to bloom in the next twenty years at every level: global, regional, local. In Part Three, we'll see an example of this at the global level: global issues networks, whose design also reflects the other two new realities of flatter, more networked organizations and of moving beyond the nation-state's traditional ways of doing things.

PART TWO

High Noon—for Twenty Urgent Global Issues

8
A Dangerous Gap

Return to one of the key graphs of Part One:

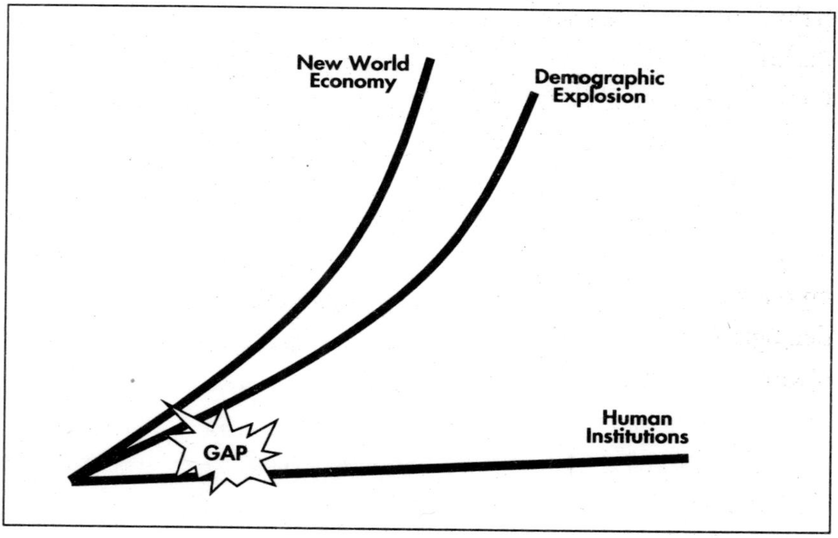

FIGURE 8.1 *The Two Big Forces—Gap*

As we saw earlier, one of the great challenges of our times is the gap that develops when the curves fly apart—when human institutions prove unable to master the stresses brought about by the exponential forces that will so dramatically change the world over the next twenty years.

What to do? Quite a few people believe that the challenge is to keep the demographic and new world economy lines from surging ahead. But as should have become apparent in Part One, this is a pipe dream.

The two forces aren't driven by intentional decisions but by powerful underlying forces—demographic patterns, an unstoppable technological revolution, and an economic revolution arising from the spread of the market system after the collapse of the twentieth century's central planning experiment. Maybe one could hold the new world economy line up just a little bit—but not a lot and not for long—and even that tiny delay would require forfeiting massive opportunities, such as trade liberalization, where the poorest countries stand to be the main beneficiaries.

Instead, the real challenge is to raise the human institutions line—that is, to raise the game of human institutions, particularly public institutions charged with governance. This implies a serious effort to rethink and reinvent them in the light of the three new realities just discussed—with their triple requirement of moving beyond traditional hierarchies, beyond the traditional nation-state ways of doing things, beyond the now untenable separation of the public, private, and civil society spheres.

This will be hard to do. Institutions, more wedded to rituals, are even more resistant to change than individuals. So we have two crises on our hands: a crisis of complexity, produced by the stresses from the demographic and new world economy lines, and a nasty twin, a crisis of governance arising from the rigidity of human institutions and from the sheer difficulty of getting the human institutions line to move up.

This is not the first time these twin crises have arisen. The integration of the Atlantic economy in the nineteenth century held out the promise of a rapid economic convergence between the United States and Europe and within Europe itself. And still, this seemingly irresistible trend led to a powerful backlash, brought about by a mixture of rising global inequalities and political instability—as Kevin O'Rourke and Jeffrey Williamson show in their study of trade, migration, and capital flows in the nineteenth-century Atlantic economy.[1]

A subsequent period demonstrates even more vividly that when too many people are left behind by economic change, and governance responses also fall behind, reaction and backlash ensue. After World War I, the pace of change picked up once more. Another round of global economic integration coincided with the growing impact of electric power on industry and the birth of the modern division of labor (Chapter 3). But this period of rapid change also came to a halt, this time through the Great Depression and World War II. Studying this backlash in 1944, the farseeing thinker Karl Polanyi suggested that too much economic and social change—too fast, and in an institutional vacuum—can lead to political backlash, autarchy, and authoritarian forms of control that can destroy liberal values and human freedoms.[2]

But Polanyi also proposed a countervision. Coming out of the crucible of World War II, he called on the postwar world to harness "regulation" and "institutions"—today, we might say governance—to the task of strengthening "freedom in a complex society." Contemporaries like the German philosopher Jürgen Habermas are also inspired by this vision: his quest for a "domestic policy on the scale of the planet" is nothing less.[3] Political scientists Joseph Nye and Robert Keohane, with their idea that the world may be evolving towards "complex interdependence," also propose a vision of global complexity in which the world becomes more peaceful and harmonious even as it becomes more plural and more changeable, and the structures of power grow more diverse.[4] Part Three of this book will explore ideas that go in this direction.

In the meantime, we have a crisis of governance on our hands. And while this crisis lasts—and even expands over the years to come, as is likely—the world will face the dangerous governance gap crudely depicted in Figure 8.1.

It is within this gap that various types of trouble have been breeding. The financial crisis of 1997–1998, and the recent Argentina and Turkey turmoil. The increasing malaise everywhere about politicians' inability to tackle the big issues. The large and vocal alliances of protesters of all stripes rallying around large international events and decrying the inability of established institutions to meet their concerns and respond to the momentous changes afoot. And worst: the glaring neglect of some twenty burning global issues, many of which must be solved well before twenty years are over. One such global issue is global terrorism, as we abruptly discovered on September 11, 2001. But it's just one of many.

9
A Bad Feeling in Your Stomach: Unsolved Global Issues

Think about the last ten years or so: if you were a rich country resident, while your national politicians worried about university fees, whether or not to adopt the euro, school prayer, limiting the workweek to a certain number of hours, family planning, election financing, and the level of interest rates, did you not at times get that bad feeling in your stomach—that some bigger planetary issues were being left unattended? Haven't you been wondering here and there about the clash between the short electoral cycles and territorial allegiance that serve as most politicians' reference system, and the longer-term and cross-border nature of the most serious issues we face on this planet?

If you've lived during that period in a developing country, you must have had similar feelings, except that the big unattended issues may have been even more vividly clear to you. Their effects were probably all around you: environmental stresses, poverty, ethnic conflict, contagious diseases, and many others. On top of that you may have felt a sense of despair, not just at the short-term horizon of politicians but also at the weakness or corruption of the political system: ever-changing governments, kleptocratic elites, ministers who boast when things go well but readily blame external aid agencies when hard choices have to be made, and other confusing behavior by those in power.

At any rate, North or South, the nagging feeling that major planetary issues are being neglected expresses itself through anguished questions. What are we doing about global warming and other assaults on the environment? Not enough. What are we doing to fight poverty worldwide and to stem the spread of new infectious diseases? Not enough. What are we doing to step up the fight against illegal drugs? Not enough. What are we doing to proactively rethink issues of trade, financial crisis management, or intellectual property rights from a global standpoint? Not enough. What are we doing to make sure that biotechnology and e-commerce don't sail way ahead of our ability to at least create some minimal global rules for them? Not enough.

Why? Because we're not doing enough to tackle the underlying problem: ineffective or slow global problem-solving, arguably the most serious casualty of the governance gap we just talked about. Quite simply, the current setup for solving global problems doesn't work. We need a better one, and fast. As we will see, global government is a non-starter. There may be alternative ideas. But before we explore them in Part Three, let's have a closer look at the global issues that this planet has to face in the next twenty years or so.

10

Twenty Global Issues, Twenty Years to Solve Them

Frustration has indeed been building, even among the experts, around the growing list of complex global issues that traditional institutions seem unable to master. A sample of such issues—examples of failures, that is—is illustrated in Figure 10.1.

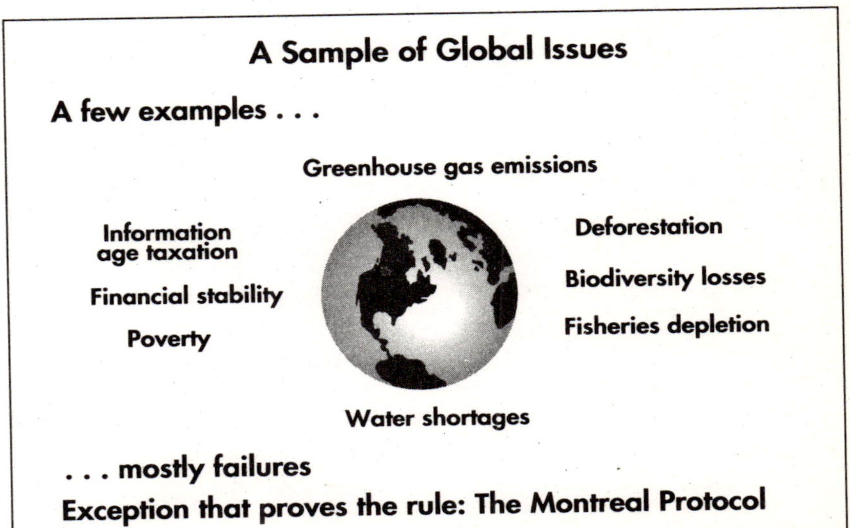

FIGURE 10.1 *A Sample of Global Issues*

Looking closer:

- Despite a near-consensus on the peril of global warming, despite the Rio 1992 Earth Summit and the 1997 Kyoto Protocol, the developed countries have made little tangible progress in curbing carbon and other greenhouse gas emissions. As talks about operational details have dragged on, many rich countries are emitting even more.[1] Following the collapse of negotiations in The Hague in November 2000, the anti-Kyoto stance of the new U.S. administration, and a watered-down last-minute deal struck without the United States in Bonn in July 2001, it is not clear if or when serious reductions in carbon emissions will set in. With the Bonn deal, recently fleshed out in Marrakesh, we will be lucky if the world's developed country group ends up reducing carbon emissions by 2015 to some 2 percent under the 1990 level, far less than the original 5-percent Kyoto target, which itself was very far from what's required.[2] The Kyoto Protocol is alive, but not well.

- Tropical forests continue to recede at 1 percent a year, with more than one-fifth cleared since 1960.

- At the current rate of biodiversity loss, one in five mammal and one in eight bird species are threatened with extinction. Despite many international efforts, extinction rates now range from 100 to 1,000 times the normal extinction rates.

- Fisheries are being depleted, with fishing capacity 100 percent above sustainable fishing. The issue is far from being solved.

- Fresh water shortages of 15–20 percent loom in much of the developing world and are already all too obvious in some stressed spots, like the Middle East. More broadly: by 2020, one person in three on the planet will suffer from water shortages. Global efforts have so far been devoted mostly to awareness-raising.

- By 2020, the number of people living on less than $2 a day may rise well over today's 3 billion unless the fight against poverty is massively stepped up. Yet rich countries have reduced official aid programs by about 30 percent over the past ten years.

- Progress on improving the global financial architecture to promote greater financial stability and reduce the likelihood of financial crises remains slow.

- The world's taxation systems could end up threatened on a major scale by the elusiveness of e-commerce, and they need redesigning for other reasons as well—but so far there has been relatively little thinking on what to do about this.

- E-commerce and biotechnology have been soaring ahead of the world's ability to come up with a minimum set of rules for them—but there has as yet been no major international effort in that direction.

The full list of global issues not properly attended to is much longer. But before going on to a more complete list, consider one effort that has worked—the international drive to phase out the substances that had opened the hole in the ozone layer that protects us from dangerous solar radiation.

Since the Montreal Protocol on Substances That Deplete the Ozone Layer was signed in 1987, the developed countries have phased out almost all production and consumption of these ozone-depleting substances—the main ones being chlorofluorocarbons. By 1999, major developing country producers such as India, China, and Russia were firmly committed to phasing out the production of these compounds. It looks like all the developing countries will meet their freeze targets and other obligations under the Protocol. Some analysts believe that the hole in the ozone layer will soon begin to shrink and that it could close completely in the next fifty years.

Why the success? Four main reasons. The concept was simply defined, and there was no ground for conflict. As someone said: "no nation could see any benefit from ozone thinning."[3] Since there are few producers, commitments were needed only from a small number of countries. The scientific base was firm, with efforts evolving in response to new scientific findings. Alternative technologies developed quickly, with strong commitments to adopt them from governments and industry all over the world, aided by special funding facilities designed to help the developing world meet the extra conversion costs.

But preserving the ozone layer is one of those exceptions that proves the rule. Most truly global issues, or as I call them "inherently global issues" (IGIs), do not lend themselves to such quick and decisive treatment, and they remain on our hands.

11
Inherently Global Issues

There may be around twenty inherently global issues, and how we deal with them over the next twenty years will determine how well the planet fares over the next generations. Just what issues are inherently global? Around mid–1999, a group in the World Bank estimated that it was involved in more than sixty "global" issues. Other agencies and institutions—such as the United Nations Development Program and the Carnegie Endowment for International Peace—are also looking at a wide range of transnational issues and governance problems.[1]

But as yet, no one has done a definitive job at defining what makes certain issues inherently global—that is, insoluble outside a framework of global collective action involving all nations of the world. Instead, many problems that aren't inherently global—air pollution or acid rain in East Asia, the kinds of malaria endemic in Africa—are rashly declared "global" when they can be tackled regionally and nationally.

Perhaps only around twenty issues may be inherently global. Within this list, there are three categories:

- The first has to do with cross-border effects and the physical confines of our living space—that is, with what people often call the "global commons." These issues have to do with how we share our planet.

- The second has to do with social and economic issues of global concern, whose solution requires the critical mass that only global coalitions can achieve. These issues have to do with how we share our humanity.

- The third deals with legal and regulatory issues that must be handled globally because of free riders and leakages. These issues have to do with how we share our rule book.[2]

Here's a glimpse at the twenty issues:

Twenty Global Issues, Twenty Years to Solve Them

Sharing our planet: Issues involving the global commons

- **Global warming**
- **Biodiversity and ecosystem losses**
- **Fisheries depletion**
- **Deforestation**
- **Water deficits**
- **Maritime safety and pollution**

Sharing our humanity: Issues requiring a global commitment

- **Massive step-up in the fight against poverty**
- **Peacekeeping, conflict prevention, combating terrorism**
- **Education for all**
- **Global infectious diseases**
- **Digital divide**
- **Natural disaster prevention and mitigation**

Sharing our rule book: Issues needing a global regulatory approach

- **Reinventing taxation for the twenty-first century**
- **Biotechnology rules**
- **Global financial architecture**
- **Illegal drugs**
- **Trade, investment, and competition rules**
- **Intellectual property rights**
- **E-commerce rules**
- **International labor and migration rules**

FIGURE 11.1 *Twenty Global Issues*

In the next three chapters, I will give just a summary of each issue, its importance, and the sort of things one could do about it—in a few pages. I will stay away from detailing, issue by issue, the history of the world's mostly failed or very limited attempts to tackle them.

Even so, to adequately summarize all twenty issues would normally require a score of experts writing separate pieces on each of them. My brief overviews are less learned, and I apologize in advance for this or that inaccuracy or unevenness that may perhaps have crept in. But they are certainly more personal and therefore more readable—you won't easily find such a unified and compact compilation anywhere else.

In any case, impatient readers ready to look at why the current international system is failing more generally—and at new ideas about global problem-solving—can jump straight to Part Three, with the option of returning to Chapters 12, 13, and 14 later.

12
Sharing Our Planet: Issues Involving the Global Commons

The global commons refers to shared things like oceans, water, forests—things we all need but that can end up abused through an implacable logic that has been called, after a 1968 article by Garrett Hardin, "the tragedy of the commons."[1] In a nutshell: in medieval Britain, a village's commons served as shared pastureland for herdsmen. For any one herdsman, to graze one more sheep produces a benefit to him of, say, +1. But there is a cost, as this additional animal will worsen the overgrazing of the commons. Because that cost, however, is shared with all the other herdsmen, it amounts to far less than –1 for our herdsman. And so he goes and adds the sheep.

And herein lies the tragedy: each herdsman has the same incentive to add sheep after sheep, until the land is so badly overgrazed that sheep raising becomes impossible. What has happened? Simply, the village community has failed to recognize that each herdsman's individual interest conflicts with the common interest. The community has failed to manage the commons from a communal standpoint.

The six global issues described below have something to do with that same failure, with the world not quite recognizing that our climate, biodiversity, forests, fisheries, fresh water resources, and oceans need to be managed from a communal, that is, global standpoint.

Global Warming

Global warming (or climate change as it is also often referred to) is rapidly emerging as one of the toughest and most threatening of the twenty or so inherently global issues. This issue is so big, so much in the limelight, that I will spend more time on it than on the others in this chapter.

The world's climate has never been static. Over the past 4.5 billion years, it has shifted constantly due to volcanic emissions, tectonic plate movements, changes in solar radiation, and several other factors. Yet, since the last ice age, the earth's climate has been relatively stable, with global temperatures varying by less than 1°C over a century in the last 10,000 years. But there is more and more evidence that human activities over the last 100 years have started to play a major role in producing rising temperature levels, with a worrisome acceleration over the last twenty years.

What's behind all this? Once solar heat reaches the earth, part of it gets absorbed by the atmosphere above us. Of the balance that hits the surface, some gets absorbed by the ground and the oceans and some bounces back. Of that bounce-back part, some escapes back into space, but some gets trapped by certain gases in the atmosphere that are forming a layer around the earth—very much as heat gets trapped inside a greenhouse. Global warming occurs when this trapping increases as a result of rising concentrations of these gases, now known as greenhouse gases:

- Carbon dioxide, emitted mostly as a result of burning fossil fuels, such as oil, gas, and coal, and also as a result of deforestation.

- Methane, mostly from cattle and rice farming and from landfill waste.

- Nitrous oxide and some other gases, including some rare and particularly vicious ones, like the industrially produced SF5 CF3.[2]

In 2001, more than a thousand of the world's top scientists (including prominent dissenters), grouped since 1988 under the Intergovernmental

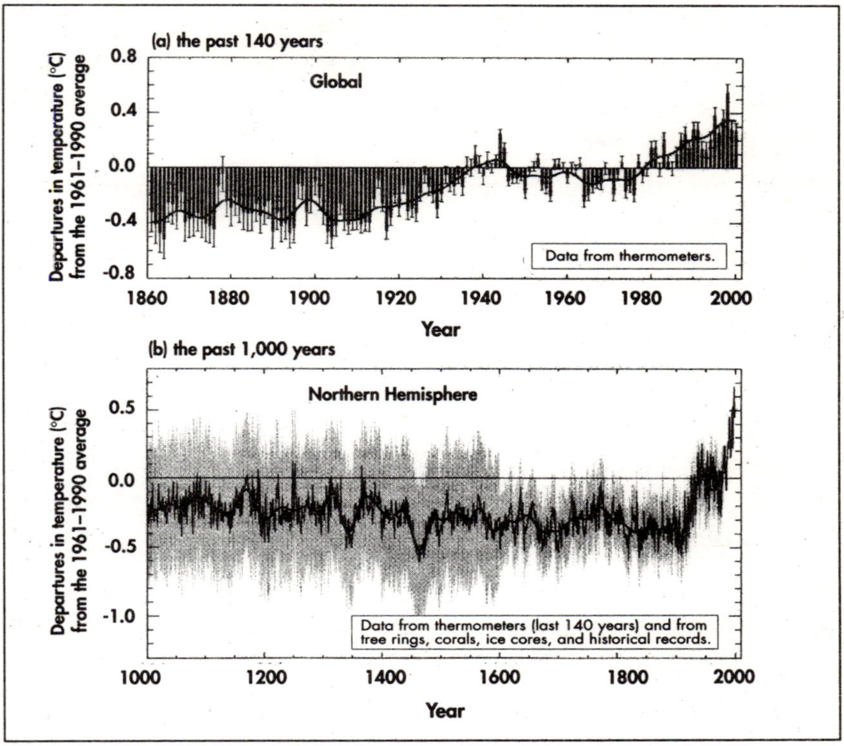

FIGURE 12.1 *Variations of the Earth's Surface Temperature. © 2001 IPCC. Used by permission.*

Panel on Climate Change (IPCC) issued a voluminous three-part report that was much more alarming than two previous reports released in 1990 and 1995.

Starting with what's already happening, the 2001 report[3] concludes that:

- The earth has warmed by about 0.6°C since 1860, with the last two decades the hottest on record.
- The increase in surface temperatures over the twentieth century exceeds that for any century, going back 1,000 years.
- Rain precipitation patterns have clearly changed, with an increase in heavy precipitations in quite a few regions of the globe.

- Ocean levels have risen 10–20 centimeters since 1900, most glaciers are retreating,[4] and the extent and thickness of Arctic ice is decreasing in summer.

- Bird migration patterns and the length of growing seasons have started to change.

- Human activities have definitely been increasing the concentrations of greenhouse gases, and most of the warming in the last fifty years is human-induced. The emission of greenhouse gases is very uneven: the United States, for instance, emits 25 percent of carbon dioxide but has only 5 percent of the world's population.

The IPCC's look into the future makes for downright scary reading. It projects that carbon dioxide, surface temperatures, rain, and ocean levels will all increase globally because of human activities:

- All the models used by the scientists project significant increases in carbon dioxide concentrations over the twenty-first century in the absence of vigorous policy changes.

- Those models predict that the earth will warm 1.4 to 5.8°C (2.5 to 10.8°F) during this century, a much higher range than that projected five years back. Land-surface temperatures will rise more than the average.[5]

- By 2100, the rise in ocean levels will range anywhere between last century's already significant increase and a whopping 80–90 centimeters—more as a result of the thermal expansion of the ocean body itself than as a result of ice melting.

- Extreme weather events will increase: heat waves, heavy downpours, floods, droughts, fires, soil moisture deficits, higher cyclone intensity, even weather-related pest outbreaks. There is a special anxiety about the possible effects of global warming on the ocean's poorly understood currents.[6] One worry among others is that the current-related "El Niño" conditions that did so much damage in recent years—from Central American floods to drought-induced forest fires in Indonesia—may start to persist.

- The length of the growing season and bird migration patterns will change even more, and plants, insects, and animals will increasingly migrate towards the poles, and upwards to higher elevations.

These changes will have major effects, lasting for generations. Billions of people will be affected directly. Some societies may be able to adapt. But poor people will be least able to do so, particularly those living in developing countries. The list of consequences includes:

- A decrease in water availability in many water-scarce regions, particularly in the subtropics.

- A decrease in agricultural productivity worldwide, especially in the tropical and subtropical regions, with the meager consolation that for small temperature increases, agricultural productivity could improve at mid- and high latitudes, mostly in richer countries.

- An increase in mortality due to heat stress, insect-borne diseases (malaria), and water-borne diseases (cholera).

- A widespread increase in the risk of flooding for tens of millions of people due to heavy rain and rising sea levels. Nearly one-third of the world's population lives within 100 kilometers of a shoreline. Places like Tuvalu, where 10,000 people live on atolls, could be wiped out,[7] as could more than 15 percent of Bangladesh's land surface. If oceans rise only 50 centimeters this century, more than 90 million people will be displaced.

- Irreversible damage to glaciers, coral reefs, atolls, mangrove systems, and polar and alpine systems—on which the livelihoods of millions depend.

Reading this list of consequences, I find it hard not to feel depressed. First, because of the sheer scope of the changes afoot and their apparent irreversibility. Even if we succeeded in stabilizing carbon dioxide concentration in this century, the IPCC scientists predict, ocean levels would still continue to rise for hundreds of years. Second, one readily suspects that the "dog years" concept (Chapter 6) applies here more than anywhere else—one year lost in addressing the problem is like seven years lost, in a manner of speaking.

Yet there is good news. There are many technological and policy options for addressing the global warming challenge, along three lines.

First, stabilization of the concentration of greenhouse gases is a must, and it is a realistic option. For example, there are known technological solutions for stabilizing carbon dioxide concentration at 450–550 parts per million (about twice the preindustrial level) in this century. This will require emissions reductions in all regions, including ten to fifteen years from now in developing countries, which by then will have exceeded the carbon emissions of rich countries. Emission ceilings for countries, regions, sectors, and firms would be one way to achieve this. An intriguing solution: assign an overall greenhouse gas concentration target and allow all countries to claim their right to share the resulting "emissions pie," with their per capita entitlements starting wide apart and then converging to equality over a predetermined period.[8]

Second, and related to this, the world will need to move towards an increasingly different energy profile. We can achieve this through higher energy efficiency (dramatically cutting the use of energy per unit of GDP); through a determined "decarbonization" of the world's energy system, meaning a massive switchover to hydropower, solar energy, and wind turbines, as well as more gas development (gas emits less carbon dioxide than oil and coal); and through innovative solutions such as underground carbon dioxide storage.

Some new technologies are especially promising. Very thin wallpaper-like solar panels could turn almost any large object into a power station, and fuel cells could act as storage devices to offset the variability of solar power. There's a huge potential for increased energy efficiency: at equal wealth, some European countries have a per capita energy consumption 50–75 percent lower than that of the United States; and many developing countries could substantially increase the energy efficiency of their industries.[9] There are some intriguing ideas around for carbon dioxide storage: for example, after stripping it from gas streams through membranes or other methods, injecting it into depleting oil fields, with a bonus of enhanced oil recovery.[10]

Taxes and tax incentives could also play a key role in getting the world to switch to a more sustainable energy profile (see Chapter 14). So will the eventual elimination of worldwide subsidies on fossil fuels, which surpass even the rich countries' astronomical agricultural subsidies and which almost always benefit mostly the well-off.

Third, forests, agricultural lands, and other ecosystems offer enormous opportunities for "sequestering" carbon dioxide, perhaps up to 200 gigatons of carbon over the next half century.

Clearly, massive changes are required, on several fronts at once—and well beyond what the Kyoto Protocol, diluted and without the United States, will achieve. Most people have a keen sense of this. What is less well known is that these changes are affordable if the problem is tackled early. The IPCC estimates that changes aimed at stabilizing carbon dioxide concentration would entail a loss of GDP between 0.2 and 2 percent—which could be brought down by half to a loss of between 0.1 and 1 percent or less through various means.[11]

The modesty of this bill is typical of all twenty inherently global issues. It is modest both in absolute terms and by comparison with the potentially enormous long-term planetary costs of leaving the issue unattended. And yet, global warming and the Kyoto Protocol provided us in Chapter 10 with the first, most glaring example of the failure by the current international setup to solve urgent global issues.

Biodiversity and Ecosystem Losses

No one knows the total number of living species, but estimates range anywhere between 10 and 15 million. What is sure is that the rate of extinction has been increasing. The main reason so many species are dying off or risking extinction is the loss of their habitats as a result of agriculture, deforestation, forest fragmentation by roads, and human population growth more generally. Other threats include global warming, pollution, hunting, fishing, trading, and the introduction of foreign species to an area.[12]

The evidence of this increased extinction rate is everywhere:

- Some 60 percent of coral reefs are threatened, a serious concern as they provide livelihoods for millions of people and the habitat for many species, including one-fourth of all marine fish.
- The world's tropical forest cover has been shrinking.
- Some 75 percent of major marine fish species are either depleted or dwindling fast due to overfishing.
- Some 50 percent of the world's coastal mangroves—vital nursery grounds for countless species—are gone.
- Nearly one in five mammal species is threatened with extinction.[13]
- One in eight bird species is at risk. The number of threatened species has doubled among penguins,[14] for example, and has quadrupled for albatross varieties.
- Hunting, habitat loss, and illegal bush-meat trade has raised the number of threatened primate species from about 100 to 120 in just a few years' time. Some conservationists fear that one or two decades from now, the Congo Basin's rain forest (the world's second-largest tropical forest) could be emptied of large mammals and that Africa's great apes could become extinct.

Amidst considerable controversy, estimates of present extinction rates range from 100 to 1,000 times the normal extinction rates, with most estimates at 1,000. And some believe that by the time mankind reaches into the next century, more than half of all species of mammals, birds, butterflies, and plants will have disappeared or will be well on their way towards extinction. As has been well said: death is one thing, but the end to birth is another.

But there's even more at stake than just preserving the wonderful and rich diversity of life on earth:

- Biodiversity plays a big role in the very stability of the five major ecosystems on which life depends: the agricultural, coastal, forest, freshwater, and grassland ecosystems.[15] A variety of plant species play essential roles at the heart of these ecosystems—from purifying water to recycling carbon and nitrogen.

- Diversity increases an ecosystem's resilience. Having more species provides a greater cushion against environmental damage, such as from global warming, drought, and other stresses. In particular, the genetic diversity of plants, insects, animals, and microorganisms determines the long-term productivity of agricultural ecosystems, their ability to bounce back after shocks, and their capacity to ensure sufficient food for the future. Yet the trend has been towards replacing polycultures with monocultures—and towards reliance on fewer varieties. Sri Lanka had 2,000 rice varieties in 1959, but by the 1980s, just five.[16]

- Biodiversity is also fundamental to human health. From high cholesterol to bacteria fighters, ten of the world's twenty-five top-selling drugs are derived from natural resources.

Biodiversity and ecosystem protection is thus one of the big and urgent global issues of the decades to come. The solutions are too complex to be laid out here, but a global framework would include many elements: protected areas, actively managed preserves, trade bans, integrated ecosystem management, certification of sustainability, seed banks, satellite monitoring, and many others. It's not that some of these haven't been tried before here and there, but it's a matter of critical mass and global resolve—and of increasing the modest resources currently devoted to conservation by a large factor.[17] Remarkably, these solutions are made more manageable and affordable by the fact that twenty-five "hot spots" covering only 1.4 percent of the planet's land area contain about 45 percent of all plant species and 35 percent of all vertebrate land animals.[18] And yet the mass extinction of species continues, despite a battery of treaties and conventions aimed at their preservation. One can say the same thing of two related issues: fisheries depletion and deforestation.

Fisheries Depletion

One of five people on this planet depends on fish as the primary source of protein. Total fish production was estimated at around 125 million tons per year in the late 1990s, worth about $70–80 billion. With the population increase and higher standards of living, demand will increase substantially. Fishing is central to the livelihoods and food security of many communities, indeed entire countries and regions. The international trade in fish and fish products is valued at about $50 billion a year.

But there is a massive problem: the viability of many fisheries and the survival of many species are threatened by overcapacity of the world's fishing fleets (about 100 percent above sustainable fishing levels) and by bad management practices (resulting, among other things, in wasting one-fourth of the sea catch). Illegal fishing could well account for 30 percent of the total production of some fisheries. And governments aren't being helpful: fishing subsidies run at close to $15 billion a year.[19]

The results: about 50 percent of marine fisheries are fully exploited, 20 percent are overexploited, and much of the rest are exploited in an unsustainable, self-destructive manner.[20] Among the major marine fish stocks—like cod and tuna—three out of four are being fished at or above their biological limit. New nets and technologies for locating schools of fish are making things worse. Some scientists even believe that despite statistics showing that the global catch has been stable or growing, it may in fact have been on the decline for a decade—in part because China may have badly overstated its production figures.[21]

These problems have encouraged the ascent of aquaculture, growing so fast in the 1990s that it now accounts for some 40 million tons, or one-third of the world's fish production. Yet it brings its own worries: chemical pollution, and biological risks as farmed fish escape and join wild communities. These concerns are increased because of the sheer range of countries, from Canada to China, that are experimenting with genetic modification programs. Another worry is the aberration of resorting to sea catch for feeding farmed fish.

Fisheries depletion is a tough issue for the world's governments. Solving it would require massive reductions in fishing fleets, stringent controls on illegal fishing and fishing practices, strictly enforced limits on the number of fish to be taken in a given period, and other politically unpalatable measures. Even the European Union (EU), with its collective approach to the issue, has so far failed to stabilize fish stocks in the North Sea. Yet the world won't solve its fisheries depletion problem without much more determined global action along these lines.

There are some radical, even surprising alternative ideas around that could facilitate global action. Scientists have noted that if you ban fishing altogether for several years in some areas, the overall catch will be increased, and in a sustainable way. In some 100 areas where such bans occurred, the number of fish increased 90 percent within a few years, their size increased 30 percent, and the number of species by 20 percent. Fascinatingly, these beneficial effects seem to spill over into adjacent areas where fishing remains permitted: in St. Lucia, for instance, one-third of the country's fishing grounds were designated no-take areas in 1995, and within three years, commercially important fish stocks had doubled in the seas adjacent to these areas. Hence the idea of creating a global network of fishing parks, with alternating bans in designated areas and constant fleet redeployments—with the added benefit that such a policy would be easy to enforce, as any fishing vessel entering a banned area could easily be tracked by satellite.[22]

Other pathbreaking ideas adopted by, for instance, New Zealand, Iceland, and parts of the United States would also be good candidates for global application. They have given fishermen rights to an assigned quota (set at a sustainable level) and have allowed them to trade the quotas freely—with the result that the stocks are reviving.[23]

As with many of the twenty burning global issues, the cost of tackling this one could be very modest on a global scale—as these ideas hint at. What's lacking is not so much resources as new approaches to global problem-solving—more on this later.

Deforestation

The same can be said for another threatening global commons issue—the loss of forest cover and the advance of deserts and savannas the world over.

Few of us realize how central a role forests play. Along with woodlands and scattered trees, forests provide the planet's population with shelter, food, fuelwood, medicines, building materials, and paper. They contribute to freshwater quality by slowing land erosion and filtering pollutants—and they regulate the timing and rate of water flow. About two-thirds of all terrestrial species are in forest areas, which are thus critical to biodiversity conservation. And when forests grow, they sequester carbon—so they are a crucial part of the fight against global warming.

What's the global situation? Today, about 30–35 million square kilometers of forests remain, or about 25 percent of the world's total land surface—probably down 20–50 percent from pre-agricultural times, though no one knows exactly.[24] Forests in industrial countries have increased slightly over the past decades, but their trees are getting younger, smaller, and less diverse.

But the real problem is in developing countries, where there are several types of issues:

- Their forests have been shrinking by more than 130,000 square kilometers (or close to 1 percent) a year. Some 20 percent of tropical and subtropical forests have disappeared since the 1960s. In

Indonesia alone, for example, deforestation has run at 17,000 to 20,000 square kilometers a year over the last decade, shrinking its forest cover more than 50 percent since 1985; at the going rate, Kalimantan's forests will disappear in nine years and Sumatra's lowland forests in four. The main reasons behind this worldwide trend are the pressure of population growth, leading to an expansion of subsistence agriculture and to unsustainable fuelwood collection; large-scale cattle ranching in Latin America; government-planned settlement schemes; and illegal logging. In Indonesia, 70 percent of log production is derived from illegal sources.[25]

- Forest fragmentation—by roads, agriculture, and logging—also has a large negative impact. It reduces the natural habitat, blocks migration routes, and opens avenues for undesirable foreign species. Roads provide access for hunting, timber harvesting, and other disturbances to the local ecosystem. And where fragments are too small to support top predators, cascade effects degrade diversity.

- Forest fires appear to be on the increase. While forest fires can be a natural and useful phenomenon, Brazilian wildfires increased 50 percent in 1996–1997, and again by 80 percent in 1997–1998. Recent giant fires in Southeast Asia caused respiratory problems for 20 million people and several billion dollars in damages—Indonesia lost 46,000 square kilometers of forest in 1997 alone.[26] The El Niño phenomenon was part of the story.

All these factors combine to turn the future of tropical and subtropical forests into an important global issue. It has several dimensions:

- Timber production has increased 50 percent since 1960. With plantations providing 20 percent of all timber, scarcity is not a global problem in itself. The worry is that the spread of tree farms hasn't reduced the pressure on natural forests. In many developing countries, trees continue to be harvested at a much faster rate than natural regrowth. Typically, once forests are cleared, the land is eventually converted to other uses, in a self-reinforcing cycle. Illegal logging by major groups and by farmers using slash-and-burn techniques is a major culprit.

- Fuelwood, along with charcoal, accounts for half the world's biomass energy use—on which 2 billion people in the developing world depend—and 30 percent of the world's total energy consumption. It is already becoming scarce in some regions, particularly near urban centers. With the coming population increase almost entirely in the developing world, fuelwood demand could easily exceed by 50 percent or so what can be sustainably supplied.

- Forest loss has eroded the capacity of the world's forests to retain and filter water, and to regulate its flow. Forests are most crucial in the watershed areas—but nearly 30 percent of those areas have lost three-fourths of their original forest cover. Since forests also tend to moderate runoff during rains and thaws, their loss makes mudslides and downstream flooding more frequent—Himalayan forest losses have made life much harder in lower-lying Bangladesh. And since they also release water during drier times, their loss also makes drought situations worse.

- As forests go, so goes biodiversity. Forests need protecting for the sake of diversity itself and because they have become a major source of new goods and services—including pharmaceuticals, industrial raw materials, and revenue-earning tourism and recreation services. Already, close to 10 percent of tree species are threatened with global extinction, and the invasion of foreign species has become a problem in many places.

- Forests store more carbon than any terrestrial ecosystem—perhaps 40 percent of all carbon is stored that way. Clearing tropical forests and burning the debris releases large amounts of carbon back into the atmosphere as carbon dioxide. Beyond large-scale forest clearing, even logging and clearing small areas of forest for agriculture significantly reduces its carbon storage capabilities. Restoring degraded forests or changing their management is a major avenue for carbon sequestration and one of the strategies for addressing global warming.

Many solutions exist, as the considerable success of plantations shows—they produce 20 percent of the world's timber on only 3 percent of the forest area. And many sustainable forestry options have been developed over the years, with the best involving local participation by villagers or, as in India's Ahmedabad, even town dwellers. We must also develop a potent certification mechanism for sustainable forestry and fight illegal logging at a global level.[27]

Deforestation is another global issue, with huge stakes for the planet, whose solution isn't that expensive or technically complex. Yet we're far from having made a real dent.

Water Deficits

Many places in the world are getting drier—not just because of climate change but also because of the demands of irrigation and industry. Lake Chad has shrunk to one-twentieth of its size in 1960.[28] The Aral Sea is about gone. The Colorado River no longer reaches the sea in the dry season. Just 10 percent of the Mesopotamian marshlands are left. Worldwide, some 2–3 billion people could face acute freshwater shortages by 2020, which translates into one person in three, compared with one in ten today. About twenty countries are now water-stressed; by 2020 there will be more than forty. Asia, sub-Saharan Africa, and even the Mediterranean will be the most affected regions. For the developing world as a whole, the shortage could average 15–20 percent, with some already tense spots, like the Middle East, much worse off.

Water scarcity will be caused mainly by increased demand and pollution, and will be aggravated by global warming:

- Irrigation, accounting for 70 percent of the world's demand for water, must increase to meet the 40 percent or so expansion of food supplies needed by 2020. It takes 1,000 times more water to grow food for an individual than to meet that person's need for drinking water. Yet more than half the water entering irrigation systems never makes it to the crops, due to leaks or wasteful practices. And excess irrigation damages lakes, rivers, and marshes—ecosystems on which many poor people depend for food, fish, and timber. In Russia and Central Asia, many major inland seas, lakes, and rivers are in terminal decline for mostly that reason.

- Pollution is another growing worry. About 97 percent of the world's freshwater stock lies underground in aquifers, with a residence time that averages 1,400 years, against sixteen for rivers. The world over, these aquifers are being either badly overused (in China, India, the western United States, and many other places) or badly polluted, generally almost irreversibly, through nitrates, pesticides, and other man-made products. In parts of northwestern France, nitrates have about ruined the aquifers. This phenomenon is probably worse than we know because it can remain invisible for a long time: pollution from nineteenth-century textile mills in Massachusetts is just starting to show up in artesian wells in Long Island.

Water deficits are thus building towards a major planetary challenge. With climate change making the problem worse, there is a strong global angle. Control over water could become a frequent cause of international conflict, particularly where there is a history of antagonism and one country has the power to restrict the flow of a crucial river.[29] The number of river basins shared by several countries has gone up from 210 or so to 260 in the last twenty years. Water shortages are also tightly connected to poverty and health issues, themselves immense global challenges.[30]

Here again, there is no dearth of technical and policy solutions to the water deficit issue—solutions that call for determined action at the global level:

- Technologies like drip irrigation, precision sprinklers, low-cost high-efficiency irrigation systems, drought-resistant varieties, and new rice irrigation systems can make an enormous difference and should become the target of urgent global technology-sharing efforts. The same applies to desalination, which is still expensive but could leap forward with the discovery of more efficient membranes and processes to remove the salt from seawater.

- Another key to improved water management has to lie in setting prices that better reflect the cost of supplying and distributing it. The World Resources Institute, the World Conservation Union (IUCN), and others strongly believe that the major cause of water scarcity and damage to freshwater ecosystems is the undervaluation of water the world over. Proper pricing may include, as in Ecuador, the cost of protecting the cloud forest from which the water springs. Some people argue that in many cases, it would help to allocate water rights and make them tradable.

- Better water management also includes helping many countries and regions with advanced techniques: modernizing irrigation systems, more systematic management of water basins, interbasin conveyance systems, and regional initiatives around shared waters—such as between the ten countries that make up the Nile Basin and whose 250 million population will grow to more than 400 million by 2020.[31]

- Water safety and sanitation require a major effort as well: today, 1 billion people lack access to safe water, and 2 billion lack sanitation. Both are directly linked to poverty and disease.[32]

- All in all, water infrastructure and management investments in the developing countries must more than double from the current $75 billion per year level,[33] requiring massive aid as governments are budget strapped and as the private sector will only finance a small share (see Chapter 13).

Water deficits are maybe a decade away from becoming a particularly ugly and dangerous global issue. There have been some useful international efforts so far, but they have focused mostly on awareness-raising and have produced little beyond calls for action. The time has come to go beyond that. The world badly needs vigorous global action, in part to make sure the technology and policy challenges are addressed more determinedly across the globe, and in part to help overcome the local opposition that some of the most-needed changes (such as pricing and allocation of water rights) will undoubtedly trigger.

Maritime Safety and Pollution

The oceans, covering some 70 percent of the planet's surface, are essential to life on earth. Yet they have been under increasing stress, and the two big forces—the population increase and the new world economy—will push them even closer to the limit in the decades to come.

Besides the impact global warming may have on ocean levels and on major currents, there are several things to worry about:

- Serious oil spills and other accidents: despite major efforts at regulating ship construction and operations, serious accidents are still on the rise. Since the *Exxon Valdez* went down in Alaska's Prince William Sound in 1989, the world has seen the equivalent of thirty *Valdez* accidents.

- Despite many international rules on sea discharge, ships increasingly release their oil and other ship waste into the sea. The booming sea tourism industry has emerged as a major culprit. Often picking the waters of countries with lax monitoring practices, cruise ships account for 80 percent of waste thrown into the ocean, from human waste and plasticware to oil and chemical releases.

- Many seas are threatened by waste and pollutants generated on land by agriculture, industries, and municipalities. An example among many: the Baltic Sea, whose ecosystem was particularly fragile to start with, has a near-lifeless seabed and scores poorly on some of the most dangerous chemicals known to man, such as dioxin.

- Hazardous waste—toxic ash, dangerous industrial sludge, contaminated medical or military equipment, old batteries, spent nuclear reactor fuel—is being shipped around in increasing amounts, much of it by sea, much of it illegally and in accident-prone conditions.

- Both legal and illegal fishing practices have been damaging the integrity of sea ecosystems in many places. Among the worst culprits are large dragnets that tear up the seabed.

You'd think that maritime safety and pollution would be among the more manageable global issues. The subissues are easily identified, and the solutions should be within reach and affordable: for example, experiments with marine sanctuaries in the Mediterranean brought a surprisingly quick revival of seemingly doomed sections of the sea, with a surge of whale and dolphin populations. And it is a global issue that has been the subject of some forty treaties and conventions. Yet the health of oceans remains an ominous, still open issue for the planet. Some rules are still lacking (there are no uniform definitions of hazardous waste, for example) and where they exist, outright violations are very common and the enforcement system very weak[34]—as is the case for many of the twenty issues.

13
Sharing Our Humanity: Issues Requiring a Global Commitment

The next six issues are entirely different from the global commons–type problems we just looked at. They involve social and economic concerns that are so urgent and pervasive that nothing less than a global commitment or coalition will solve them. They bring up the idea of burden-sharing, or global solidarity.

Massive Step-Up in the Fight Against Poverty

Reducing world poverty is arguably the main global challenge of the next twenty years. Why? First, for moral reasons, and for the sake of justice and balance. A world where less than 20 percent of the people consume 85 percent of the goods and services just isn't tenable—and will become even less so as we grow from 6 billion to about 8 billion people in the first quarter of this century. As Martin Wolf of the *Financial Times* vividly puts it: "Think of a stretch limousine driving through an urban ghetto. Inside is the post-industrial world of Western Europe, North America, Australasia, Japan, and the emerging Pacific Rim. Outside are all the rest."[1] What's more, the pampered global elite in the limousine, which represented 30 percent of the world population in 1950, will be down to less than 15 percent by 2020.

But there is yet another reason to see poverty as the planet's number one challenge: it connects with many other global issues on our list, and if we don't succeed in reducing it substantially, solving the other problems becomes even harder. Poverty and distress are a breeding ground for disease, environmental degradation, internal conflict, and terrorism. Conversely, if poverty decreases massively over the next twenty years, many other good things will happen—like all six issues in this chapter, it is an "underlier" issue.

Where is poverty today?[2] There is some good news. We have cut the rate of absolute poverty—people living on less than $1 a day—from 29 percent of the world's population in 1990 to 23 percent in 1999.[3] Of course, because population increased by 1 billion during the last decade, the absolute numbers were less striking: 100 million people were lifted above the $1 a day since 1990. But the reduction in the total number of extremely poor people is nevertheless unmistakable. It was due in large part to China's 7–8 percent growth rate in the 1990s, which enabled it to bring the absolute poor in its territory down from 360 million to some 200 million. Even some African countries have grown at high rates and made substantial progress—Cape Verde, Mozambique, Uganda, Botswana.

Clearly, poverty can be reduced, and fast. For the first time in centuries, countries can double or triple their living standards within a single generation, as many Asian, Latin American, and even African countries have shown. The champion, Korea, went from a per capita income of $300 to $8,500 in a little more than one generation. Countries as diverse as Botswana, Chile, and Thailand have doubled their per capita incomes in ten years. More broadly, the overall developing country group has seen life expectancy rise from forty-five to sixty-five years and literacy rates rise from 55 percent to 75 percent, all since the early 1970s. The average speed of development in large parts of the developing world has been two to three times that of the rich countries around the middle of the nineteenth century.

But there's also bad news. There are still 1.2 billion people living in abject poverty on less than $1 a day—65 percent of them in Asia and 25 percent in Africa, where most live on less than 60 cents a day. Worldwide, close to 3 billion people—half the world's population—live on less than $2 a day. Everywhere, the worst affected are children, women, and old people. More than 800 million people suffer from hunger and malnutrition.[4] Global poverty is shockingly deep and widespread.

It has become clear that poverty means more than lack of income: it includes isolation and powerlessness, insecurity, lack of services, and lack of control over one's future. It means spending hours every day gathering water and fuelwood, suffering from indoor pollution, facing domestic violence, being mistreated by police and government officials, and feeling constantly exposed to catastrophic risks—such as just one family member becoming ill.[5]

Where will poverty be tomorrow? There is an internationally agreed target of halving poverty by 2015—a tall order considering five complicating factors:

- The population increase, from 6 to about 8 billion by 2020–2025, with more than 95 percent of the increase coming in the developing countries, may well under current trends increase the world poverty numbers.

- Due to the population growth and the youthfulness characteristics of the developing world, the average economic growth rate needed year after year to make a serious dent into poverty is 5–6 percent, much higher than the average 3.5 percent scored by the developing countries in the 1990s. This fact hasn't sunk in with many people yet.

- Increasing disparities within countries—already observed in Latin America since the 1980s but now a more general phenomenon—may complicate the task of reducing poverty.[6] What's needed is not just strong growth, but the right kind of growth—the kind that also reduces inequality and empowers the poor to use their main asset, their labor.[7]

- There will also be the aggravating influence of many of the other global issues to reckon with—including many of the environmental ones discussed above, which hurt the poor the most if they remain unsolved.

- Even under optimistic scenarios, Africa will remain the most challenging case. One reason is the very high level of accumulated social and economic distress in many countries of that region, and eroding prices for the commodities they export. Others include AIDS and malaria, the ethnic conflicts and internal wars that affect one African in five, and the pervasiveness of bad government and corrupt elites.

Looking forward, the challenge is enormous—requiring nothing short of a massive step-up in the fight against poverty, especially in Africa. Yet rich countries chose to reduce their official aid by nearly 30 percent since the early 1990s. For the fifty or so "least developed countries" (mostly located in Africa), rich governments have reduced their aid from $17 billion in 1990 to $12 billion today—yet those countries account for 10 percent of the world's people and represent the hard core of poverty. Rich countries have pledged in 1970 to provide official development aid equal to 0.7 percent of their GDP.[8] In effect, their aid peaked at 0.35 percent of their GDP in 1990 and had fallen by 2000 to a 0.22 percent average, with the United States at 0.10 percent.

There are all kinds of reasons for this. The complacency that followed the fall of the Berlin Wall. Doubts about the effectiveness of aid. And a public, such as in the United States, which stubbornly believes aid to be a huge multiple of its actual amount.

Yet many pieces have been falling into place to create an environment in which aid can be much more effective than its partially successful, partially frustrating record of the past thirty years:

- The official aid approach is shifting to a new model that has shown to be productive in the more than a dozen countries where it is being tried out. That model, which runs under various IMF, World Bank, and United Nations labels, is quite different from the past one. Countries themselves take ownership of their own development and poverty reduction strategies. Governments consult civil society, business, and all foreign agencies as they formulate these strategies. They lay them out transparently, sector by sector, with performance indicators, and over a time frame that spans electoral cycles. And they coax foreign agencies, NGOs, and others into adopting a partnership and division-of-labor approach around them. Complementing this, aid is shifted away from self-standing projects towards more flexible funding at the level of the national budget or of the sector budget (e.g., the education budget). The new model also takes into account the broader definition of poverty—beyond just income poverty—and puts a lot of emphasis on empowerment.

- There are new, powerful ideas for improving aid allocation. Crude but eye-opening research shows that aid has a positive impact in countries that follow sound policies in the first place, but zero or even negative impact in those that don't.[9] This suggests that aid will pull up to three times more people out of poverty every year if it is deployed mostly on poor people living in countries with good policy environments than if it is spread around indiscriminately across many countries. Of course, this creates terrible dilemmas for aid agencies: what to do about very poor, distressed people in poorly run countries? But the implications for successful poverty reduction are clear, and readily actionable.

- Aid harmonization also holds the promise of higher aid effectiveness, to the point of saving the beneficiary countries at least 20 percent of the amount donated or lent—through lower transaction and procurement costs. Without such harmonization efforts, the average African country has to deal with 600 projects at any given time, receives 1,000 official visits a year, and writes 2,400 reports each quarter for the aid agencies or NGOs that sponsored the projects. This problem—along with costly habits of tying procurement to national suppliers of each donor country—is now being seriously addressed by national (bilateral) and multilateral aid authorities.

- Four critical areas are increasingly being targeted by aid programs to help the receiving countries lift their own game: good governance, the business climate, education, and connectivity. All four areas are high-leverage—addressing them enables many other efforts to succeed where they would otherwise fail. Good governance and the eradication of corruption are the prerequisites for many other things to happen. They require a decent civil service, honest judges, the rule of law, independent supervisory authorities, parliamentary oversight—even good investigative journalists. A good business climate is essential to the 5–6 percent growth rates that massive poverty reduction demands in much of the developing world; it means acting on some fifty items, from sound banking through customs cleanups to microfinance.[10] (I will discuss education and connectivity below.)

Together, these changes represent a quiet revolution in aid and poverty reduction programs. They could double or triple the impact of aid in the decades to come. But that quiet revolution is less than halfway engaged. There still is a major need for global action to push thousands of bilateral, multilateral, and NGO donors towards really working together along these new lines, with the developing countries in the driver's seat and owning up to their own responsibilities. The best clients are the poor themselves: when they participate and take ownership of the programs that affect them, the effectiveness of those programs soars. In India, when people are alerted about the sums sent to their village for education or sanitation programs and asked to monitor the expenditures, the amount of money that actually serves the intended use is dramatically higher.

But raising the effectiveness of aid through this quiet, qualitative revolution is just one part of the global poverty challenge. The other one, without which the required massive reduction in poverty is unlikely to happen, is the quantitative challenge of channeling more resources from the rich to the developing countries. Official aid has shrunk to $55 billion a year, yet far more than this is required to get the job done, even in a high-effectiveness aid environment.

If the rich countries honored their pledge to devote 0.7 percent of their GDP to aid, $100 billion more would be available each year. A brave group of European countries—affectionately called the G0.7 and including the Netherlands, Sweden, Denmark, Norway, and Luxembourg—has shown it can be done by even exceeding this target. In addition, if the rich countries opened their markets more widely to the exports of poor countries and reduced the enormous subsidies to their own agriculture, this would be worth at least another $50–100 billion a year to the developing world—a tremendous boon for serious poverty reduction, even though not every increase in trade helps every poor person.

Even if the rich world stopped halfway on these two aid and trade items, some $75–100 billion more would accrue every year to the developing countries. This magnitude would put the world on track towards a serious step-up in the fight against poverty.

For perspective, compare these sums with:

- the *one-off* $30 billion debt-relief package for the poorest, most highly indebted countries, launched in 1998 by the G7 and talked about almost to the exclusion of anything else;

- the peace dividend of $400 billion *a year* in defense savings realized worldwide between 1987 and today—with rich countries having cashed in 70 percent of these savings;[11] and

- the $360 billion *a year* that rich countries spend subsidizing their own agriculture.

This issue—fighting poverty in a major, definitive way—is truly global: it requires joint efforts by developed and developing countries. Not only is solving it the acid test for our ability to share our humanity, but it is also the test for how serious we are about solving global issues at large. Poverty is the top issue because it underlies many of the others. Fail on this one, fail on everything.

Peacekeeping, Conflict Prevention, and Combating Terrorism

Wars between states have given way almost entirely to *intrastate wars and armed conflicts*. In 1999–2000 there were no fewer than fifty such wars, and they had killed 7 million civilians since their inception. More than 90 percent of them since 1945 have taken place in developing countries. These conflicts increasingly draw surrounding countries into the violence: the civil war in the Democratic Republic of Congo spurred a regional war involving seven other countries, and the conflicts in Sierra Leone, Liberia, and Guinea-Bissau have also become intertwined.

The cost is staggering. The Congo regional war, the deadliest since World War II, is estimated to have killed 2 million or more. Africa has so many wars that one person in five is affected by them. In some places, children have a 75 percent chance of dying before they are two years of age. Years of development are being reversed, and roaming armies are spreading AIDS. But Africa isn't alone: there have been almost as many conflicts in Asia, and quite a few in other regions, including the former Yugoslavia zone.

Terrorism, long a part of internal conflicts, in the 1970s became a wider phenomenon that spread by imitation, even outside intrastate wars. National counterterrorist measures were promptly taken to eliminate such groups as the Baader-Meinhoff gang in Germany, the Red Brigades in Italy, and Action Directe in France. Similar efforts are being directed at the Basque separatists' ETA movement and at the IRA.

But over the last decade terrorism has gone global, largely circumventing national controls, in two ways. First, it has, as exemplified by the Al-Qaeda terrorist group, created exactly the sort of flat, networked, worldwide organization that is such a hallmark of the age to come, in effect trumping more traditional, hierarchical national antiterrorist organizations. Second, it has sought refuge in failed states, like Afghanistan, Somalia, and other territories outside the control of any recognized government.

The reach and destructiveness of global terrorism became clear on September 11, 2001. Thousands of people from eighty nations died in New York, Washington, and Pennsylvania, altering for decades the world's image of itself—and of its future. Beyond the toll in life and property in the United States, the ensuing worldwide reduction in growth, commodity prices, tourism receipts, and financing possibilities has probably caused 10 million people in the developing world to slip under the line of extreme poverty (half of them in Africa) and has led to the death of 20,000 to 40,000 more children under five years of age, as a result of a setback in the fight against malnutrition and diseases. Clearly, global terrorism has joined intrastate wars and armed conflicts on the list of destructive disruptions of peace whose solution requires a global commitment.

There have been three kinds of responses to these various types of disruptions:

- United Nations peacekeeping efforts in 2000 involved some 40,000 soldiers, observers, and police, twice as many as in 1999. They come from ninety countries and involve a great number of nations: only 10 percent of the personnel deployed are from the five permanent UN Security Council members—the United States, the United Kingdom, France, China, and Russia.

- Wars of intervention, as they have come to be called, include the messy, costly but eventually successful Kosovo intervention, the quick episode in East Timor, and a not-so-successful intervention in Sierra Leone.

- The beginnings of global efforts against global terrorism include a dozen UN conventions (even though as of September 2001, few countries were party to them), and some new measures.

Here again, we have another global issue that's only partially solved—from three standpoints.

First, the *peacekeeping and intervention* setup is actually quite fragile and needs several improvements that require global thinking:

- *Means*. Unpaid peacekeeping dues, $2 billion or so in mid–2001, keep the UN teetering close to bankruptcy. Late in 2000, the UN had enough cash to keep peacekeeping going for only three months. It also badly needs more staff, equipment, and information-gathering capabilities.

- *Quicker responses*. Conflicts are more easily controlled if peacekeeping kicks in early. To field missions faster, the UN's standby system needs bolstering by "on-call" lists of military officers, civilian police, judicial experts, even human rights experts. Among other things, it has been suggested that small teams of seasoned military officers from various nations be stationed at UN headquarters, ready to hit the ground running in case the Security Council approves a mission.[12] And the links with more action-ready organizations such as NATO, which increasingly plays a peacekeeping role, need to be thought through.

- *Technology*. In the United States, proponents of rethinking the military structure have a vision of smaller, more mobile units operating with more strategic attacks on vital systems, along with a flatter command structure. Such an option is especially relevant to global peacekeeping because it could enhance the effectiveness of intervention. It could also solve the intervening countries' dilemma: their need to intervene with increasingly capable opponents versus their aversion to casualties and large outlays.

- *Principles*. Unlike peacekeeping, wars of intervention lack a simple, straightforward, and widely accepted set of rules. If they are to be a serious part of tomorrow's global agenda, they'll need this sooner rather than later. Otherwise chaos could well set in.[13]

Second, the best method is *conflict prevention* in the first place—something the world hasn't been good at. Prevention is thus another area requiring serious global thinking and action. A World Bank analysis of some eighty intrastate conflicts shows that they predominantly occur where rebel organizations are financially viable. Liberation movements based on genuine grievance exist, but most only use that cover to get their hands on some valuable resource—it's more a story of greed than grievance.[14] In fact, the research shows that internal conflicts are very likely in countries:

- where incomes are very low, and where the level of education is low, too—again, poverty connects to just about everything;
- where an exportable resource can be captured and easily cashed in (petroleum, diamonds, drugs);
- where one large ethnic group dominates smaller ones (when there are many small groups, the risk goes down); and
- where there are large diasporas abroad—wealthier expatriate nationals are often responsible for refueling a civil war after it has been stopped.

By focusing directly on these factors, we can tilt global action towards preventing conflicts rather than mostly waiting to intervene once they have started. There are several ways to do this:

- Through international tracking of the looted resource—such as "conflict diamonds"—to make it harder to sell.
- Through intensifying the fight against money laundering, with direct and early seizures of assets belonging to leaders of predator movements (just as governments have started to do for terrorist networks).
- Through special global efforts to control the small-arms trade in countries with a high likelihood for conflict based on the above factors.

- Through special conflict-prevention efforts and human rights watching briefs over countries where one large group dominates another—including pushing to entrench the rights of minorities in the constitution.

Third, the *fight against global terrorism,* now clearly a major new agenda item for the world, has only begun and will take many years. How global an issue this has become can be seen from the extraordinarily large number of nations (more than fifty) in which a group like the Al-Qaeda network operates; from its ability to bury loosely connected sleeper cells deep into societies; and from the large range of countries (some two dozen) in which it has tried to start destabilizing operations—from the United States to Jordan to Ecuador and even Singapore. Combating such networks will require an unprecedented step-up in the global sharing of intelligence, in the global conduct of prosecutorial work, and in formulating shared operational definitions and criteria. As was mentioned above, one of the things to do is to step up the fight against money laundering and against other uses of financial channels to support terrorism—an issue taken up in the next chapter. Another proposal is a possible "refoundation" of NATO, perhaps including Russia and China, around the related tasks of countering terrorism and weapons of mass destruction.[15]

Like other global issues, addressing the threesome of peacekeeping, conflict prevention, and fighting global terrorism comes only at a modest cost. Peacekeeping efforts by the UN have cost only $30 billion since such operations began in 1948. Global efforts aimed at conflict prevention would cost even less—and would avoid massive human distress and societal disruption. And combating global terrorism, while it will carry a higher price tag than anyone would have guessed before September 11, 2001, has more to do with global organization than huge expenditures. For example, tracking down terrorism finance involves doing more of what we should have been doing all along to combat financial abuse and money laundering (see Chapter 14).

And it has to do with changing two mindsets. First, changing the mindset that led the world to lower its guard after the fall of the Berlin

Wall, leaving the global community, as someone said, "without adult supervision" in an age where technology permits small terrorist networks, warlords, and rebel groups to have the impact once available only to large national armies. Second, changing the mindset that has allowed excessively compartmentalized subcultures of specialists to sprout around issues like terrorism, peacekeeping, conflict prevention, nuclear nonproliferation, and so on, when what's needed is a more unified approach to global security that better integrates these sub-issues and subcultures.

Education for All

One in six adults on the planet cannot read or write. Some 600 million women and 300 million men, 99 percent of them in the developing countries, remain illiterate. Some 115 million children between six and eleven—one in five—are not in school. Of those who go to school, one in four drops out before completing five years of basic education—when research shows that adults with less than five to six years of education remain non-numerate and functionally illiterate. South Asia, Africa, and the Middle East are the three regions where these problems are most severe.

Moreover, throughout the developing world, the quality of primary, secondary, and university education is rarely up to the standards required by the new world economy. And globally, we're far away from seeing the emergence of a badly needed system of international accreditation.

Why is education a global issue when so much of it happens locally, and when the main problems are concentrated in the developing world? The answer is fourfold:

- Education is central to the construction of genuinely democratic societies. Even from a moral standpoint, one could argue that education is a kind of universal right because it provides "human capabilities," in the words of economist Amartya Sen—the essential and individual power to reflect, make choices, and steer towards a better life.

- Education is key to building the sense of global citizenship that global problem-solving requires—as Part Three will hint at. And it is a major tool for developing a sense of shared global values that may help spare the next generations unnecessary, obsolete tensions between civilizations.

- Education is one of the most powerful instruments for reducing poverty and inequality and for laying the basis for sustainable growth. It has strong links not just to productivity growth but to improved health, to the ability to understand the need to care for the natural environment, and even to population stabilization. Girls' education, for example, brings one of the highest returns known in the field of economic development. So education, like poverty, is an "underlier" issue par excellence, and both are strongly linked. Other global issues will be easier to solve if education is successfully tackled at a global scale.

- Finally, the new world economy, with its knowledge intensity, requires a leap forward in each country's education effort—from primary to higher education, and even to lifelong learning and the accreditation of competencies. If that does not happen in a very large number of countries, expect even greater inequalities between countries over the decades to come. Research shows that until a country's population reaches a threshold of about six years of schooling on average, it remains trapped in a low-return economy prone to bad governance—and the new world economy is sure to bump this threshold up some more over the next twenty years. Globally, education can either be a great equalizer or a great divider.

So what's to be done? An agenda to deliver global education for all would include several items.

A first urgent global task is to help build or rebuild basic education worldwide. Except in two regions, Central Asia and West Africa, the average share of primary education in national budgets has increased over the past two decades. Yet there is much unfinished business. In the developing world, the quality of basic education is often very low due to the lack of adequate facilities, competent teachers, textbooks, parental support, and community involvement. Even where enrollment numbers are good, dropout and class repetition rates are often very high.

More resources are thus urgently required to boost both the quantity and quality of basic education in the developing world. How much would that cost? Not much from a global standpoint: some $10–15 billion a year for basic education. But much of this must come from official aid. School fees are not a good idea. And government budgets cannot handle the step-up alone: in Nepal, to take an example, it would mean increasing educational expenses from 13 percent to 17 percent of an already tight national budget.

But strengthening basic education globally (often referred to under an "education for all" label narrower than the one I am using here) is just the first critical step. The broader strategy calls for helping as many countries as possible raise the game of their entire education system, all the way up to secondary and university education, to meet the demands of the new world economy. An international effort on this would pay off tremendously in fighting global poverty and increasing disparities. On average, one more year of basic education buys an increase in a country's growth rate of 0.4 percent, but one move up the science score ladder (by one standard deviation) raises it a full 1 percent.[16]

Finally, a global effort is also glaringly needed in setting up worldwide, cross-border accreditation systems, not for degrees, but for real-life competencies and skills. Such systems are beginning to appear in some narrow fields, such as software programming. The potential for generalizing this to many fields is enormous—and within reach, thanks to the new information and communications technologies. In a world of increasing migration, this is almost a no-brainer—yet the world has done little to launch a global, organized effort around this important idea.[17]

Education for all, in the broad sense just described, is an important global issue with strong win-win aspects. The bill would not be large on a global scale, and in this field, you would expect international collaboration and exchanges of ideas to come naturally. Yet education for all is being badly neglected. An intergovernmental conference in Dakar, Senegal, in 2000 concluded that the world had made far less progress than contemplated in an earlier such conference held ten years before in Thailand; and even then, the focus was almost entirely on basic education—-important, but only a start.

Global Infectious Diseases

The world suddenly faces an appalling health crisis. Once more, it originates largely in poverty and destitution—in the developing world. AIDS, malaria, tuberculosis, pneumonia, diarrhea, and measles now kill 13 million people a year, and the numbers keep going up. They threaten to reverse decades of development in many developing countries. They know no borders and spread faster than ever: for perspective, consider that at the end of World War I, swine flu circled the world five times in eighteen months, when commercial air traffic did not even exist.[18] Imagine how fleet-footed diseases have become now. AIDS, malaria, and tuberculosis are especially challenging.[19]

Today, 40 million people are infected by *AIDS*,[20] 95 percent of them in developing countries, 28 million in Africa alone. Since the epidemic started, twenty or so years ago, more than 60 million have been infected, and 25 million have died—close to the toll of the Black Death between 1347 and 1352 in Europe.[21] Every day, 15,000 get infected, most of them between the ages of fifteen and twenty-four. The spread of AIDS has slowed in Africa—in part because the virus encounters fewer uninfected people—but it is now accelerating in India, Russia,[22] the Caribbean, and lately China.[23] In Africa it's often spread by roaming armies, in Russia by intravenous drug users, in India by truckers, in Thailand by inmates sharing needles while in prison, in Myanmar by poor monks sharing one razor blade—the disease always finds its carriers. Prostitution and unsafe sex are always part of the equation.

Some 12 million children have been orphaned by AIDS, a figure projected to balloon to 40 million by 2010. Life expectancy, which had inched up about twenty years in many places in Africa and elsewhere over the last thirty years, has abruptly declined—by an average of six to seven years in Africa, and by more than ten years in South Africa and well-managed Botswana. In South Africa, for example, 4 to 7 million could die in this decade alone if no effective treatment is provided.[24]

More than sixteen African countries have incidence rates exceeding 10 percent of the adult population. When those rates reach 20 percent or more—as they have in some seven countries—the loss of annual income can exceed 1 percent of GDP. A downward spiral sets in. The disease strikes at young, sexually active people who would be the core of the labor force of tomorrow.[25] In some countries, already fragile civil services get depleted fast, and one of the worst casualties has been in education. In Côte d'Ivoire, AIDS has been responsible for 70 percent of the deaths among teachers. In some countries, as many teachers die from AIDS as retire or are trained annually.

Malaria, caused by a mosquito-borne parasite, is preventable but remains one of the great challenges of our times. Almost 2 billion people are affected in one way or another by the disease and its fallout, and the situation is getting worse. There are now some 300 to 500 million clinical cases a year, 90 percent in sub-Saharan Africa. One million people die from it every year. And in Africa, malaria inflicts an even greater disease burden than AIDS. Without malaria, Africa's GDP could well be $100 billion higher. But even outside Africa—in Asia, Latin America, even Eastern Europe—the malaria situation is getting worse.

Why the flare-up? Because of the debilitated health systems in Africa—now also massively burdened by AIDS—and the disease's new resistance to drugs, reported all over the world.

Even *tuberculosis*—caused by bacteria spread mostly by already infected people's coughing—is making a comeback, fifty years after the discovery of drugs that can cure it. It is on the rise all over the developing world—and now is increasing again even in rich countries, where half the cases are among the foreign-born population. There are now 8–10 million new cases of tuberculosis a year, with the major increase registered in African populations heavily affected by AIDS, but with the greatest absolute burden in Asia. About 2 million people die from it each year, and the disease costs the world some $12 billion annually in lost income. After decades of successful control, country after country is slipping back, with Peru one of the most spectacular cases.

Why so? Again, partly because health systems are being cluster-bombed by so many diseases at once, and partly because of the emergence of drug-resistant strains.

The agenda for global action has numerous parts, many of which have received intense international discussion—but timid effort:

- We need to strengthen the health systems in many developing countries. This won't be possible from local resources alone and is yet another reason for thinking big with respect to official aid. Better health promotion and prevention are important in this—considering the stark fact that treatment for AIDS, even at reduced drug prices, costs thirty times the average $10–15 per inhabitant that the poorest developing countries can typically afford to spend on their health systems.

- We need special emergency funds to prevent and treat the three diseases. The G7 group of leading countries, together with some partner countries and private donors, did just that at the 2001 Genoa summit, but at a level (about $2 billion for a first go) far below the real needs. The total financing needed to curb these three diseases is on the order of $5–7 billion a year over twenty years, and possibly much more.[26]

- Part of these resources should be used to make advance purchase commitments at a global level for new, more effective products, so as to give laboratories a bigger incentive to develop them. Today, their incentives are all stacked towards research on noncommunicable diseases in rich countries.

- For that reason, we also need to create tax incentives in rich countries to encourage development and clinical testing of these products, and to remove blockages to their marketing in poor countries.

- We may have to come up with tiered drug-pricing systems and rethink licensing rules so as to strike the difficult balance between making products more affordable and not wrecking the laboratories' motivation for developing them in the first place—a typical dilemma in the area of intellectual property rights (see Chapter 14).

- We may need to construct a new global public health approach that focuses on the good of the global public as such, above and beyond country concerns and the primacy given to individual health.[27]

Infectious diseases have become one of the world's most urgent issues. We are in a race against time to control the spread of the most dangerous diseases, before the diseases wear down the drugs themselves. Though much of it is centered on Africa, infectious disease is an inherently global issue, and like poverty and education, is an "underlier" issue—failing to solve it sets back the solution of other issues. And as some of the figures above show, the cost of resolution is again modest in global terms.[28]

The Digital Divide

Just as education can equalize or divide countries and people, information and communications technologies can go either way. Right now, these technologies—even though they have sometimes advanced surprisingly in some developing countries (Chapter 4)—are very unevenly distributed. The resulting "digital divide" is of great concern.

One consequence of the investment binge of the last few years is an unbelievable overcapacity in the world's *communications* system. If the world's 6 billion people were to talk nonstop on the phone for the next year, their words could be transmitted in a few hours through the currently available bandwidth—the capacity that connects homes and offices to each other and to providers of data all over the world.

Yet some 2 billion people have never made a phone call. Cities like Manhattan and Tokyo have more telephone lines than all of sub-Saharan

Africa. Cellular phone networks cover only 20 percent of the earth, mostly in rich countries. The telephone density (phone lines per 100 inhabitants) is fifty to sixty in rich countries but less than two in the poorest developing countries. Even among developing countries, the distribution of telecommunications is skewed: in 1999, ten large developing countries accounted for 80 percent of foreign investment in the sector. Within countries, there are equally wide disparities: in Nepal, urban homes are 100 times more likely to have phones than rural ones.

Information technology is even more unevenly distributed. The Internet traffic between the United States and Europe is 100 times that reaching Africa, and thirty times that reaching Latin America. About 10 percent of the world population understands English, the language of 75 percent of all web sites. Rich countries have 95 percent of all Internet hosts, Africa only 0.25 percent. This has something to do with low telephone density: with less than five telephones per 100, it is next to impossible for a country to leap into serious, countrywide Internet connectivity.[29]

Why should we worry about this? Because these technologies offer tremendous leapfrogging possibilities for developing countries—in so many areas that it has become hard to imagine a country developing and reducing its poverty levels without them:

- *Reducing isolation*. Cellular telephony in Bangladesh shows how a single cellular phone per village can become a real business, and a lifeline. Over the Andes, satellites providing telephony in rural areas cut down communication costs dramatically compared to the slow postal system.

- *Education*. New technologies enable teacher training and networking that raise the quality of basic education. Kids learn elementary computer skills by trial and error through "computers-in-the-wall" in Indian slums. Business schools reach hundreds of remote sites through interactive distance education in South Africa. And recall the Monterrey Tech example from Chapter 5.

- *Electronic government.* This breakthrough application is spreading fast and holds great promise for improving services to people and for cutting down opacity, bureaucratic hassle, errors and fraud. In Mauritania, an improved budget-management system paid for itself in a few months. The government system of the Indian state Andhra Pradesh is being computerized, with massive gains in efficiency and transparency.

- *Medicine.* The applications of information technology to health cover a large range—patient information, training of nurses, hygiene instructions, and even, in some cases, remote diagnostics. Data collected by remote sensors along 50,000 kilometers of African rivers have helped get river blindness under control.

- *Environmental management and ecologically balanced agriculture.* Internet-based networking, satellite detection, and best-practice exchanges can bring rapid progress in these two areas.

- *Enterprise connectivity.* Even small businesses in the developing world can hook up to their markets and their larger partners in rich countries. Recall the Moroccan garment maker and the Ethiopian goat farmer in Chapters 4 and 5.

I could go on and on.[30] In short, new technologies have become one of the most potent ways to accelerate development and reduce poverty in ways no one could have thought of even ten years ago. But from a global standpoint, it's also a matter of making sure that these technologies narrow the wealth and income gap—as opposed to letting their currently highly uneven distribution degenerate into what Berkeley professor Manuel Castells calls "technological apartheid." Given the speed of the new technologies' spread in rich countries, this is a global issue of some urgency. There is a lot of catching up to do.

And it's not an issue that calls for expensive solutions. Addressing it does not mean showering poor countries with donated phones and PCs. It means helping them develop themselves into plugged-in, savvy users of the new technologies. The kinds of global measures to consider are as follows:

- Help more than 100 developing countries rapidly develop the policies that will facilitate their transformation into knowledge-based societies across all the dimensions, from education to information infrastructure to research and innovation.

- Generalize the Chilean technique of tying private-sector investment in expanded telecommunications to remote area coverage—perhaps providing a global subsidy fund for the purpose (see Chapter 3).

- Tilt aid programs far more towards basic connectivity—including financing community communications centers in small towns and villages—and towards higher computer density and literacy levels.

- Provide a global best-practice exchange capability on the whole range of promising applications of the new technologies in developing country settings.

- Set up global North-South enterprise incubation and mentoring systems that can kick in fast. This is important because experience in Brazil and elsewhere shows that beyond sheer connectivity and Internet access, for countries to take off they need to develop a whole mesh of small companies, Internet service providers, and local content producers.

- Promote the use of the new technologies in other global issues areas, such as infectious diseases, education for all, and natural disaster prevention.

One could argue that this as yet largely unfulfilled agenda—parts of which were discussed at the G7's Okinawa and Genoa summits in 2000 and 2001—isn't at the same level of global urgency as other issues on the list of twenty. That would be a misreading. Like many issues of the second category, it's a powerful "underlier" issue, whose solution facilitates addressing other issues.

Natural Disaster Prevention and Mitigation

During the 1990s, natural disasters—floods, droughts, earthquakes, storms, strong winds, torrential rains, and mudslides—hit the world 500–800 times a year and cost more than $600 billion, more than in the previous four decades combined. Losses in the 1990s were three times those in the 1980s and fifteen times those of the 1950s. Some 45 percent of the losses in the 1990s were in Asia, 30 percent in the United States, and 10 percent in Europe. They affected some 2 billion people worldwide and killed 400,000–500,000, more than two-thirds in Asia. Half the deaths were from floods, with earthquakes the next-largest killer.

What accounts for the rise?

- Many ecosystems are now so frayed that they no longer play their natural cushioning role—deforestation and wetland destruction are examples. Dams and levees often disturb the flow of rivers and increase the severity of droughts and floods.

- People migrate to the more disaster-prone coastal zones—some 2 billion people now live within 100 kilometers of the seashore.

- More than half the world's people will soon be living in cities, and as built areas increase, losses and casualties increase as well. Many new city-dwellers live on vulnerable hillsides and floodplains.

- Global warming is making things much worse. Insurers predict huge losses from climate change on top of today's already higher loss base.

The issue has taken on such proportions and brings so much suffering that global disaster prevention and mitigation measures seem to be a must. Yet here's another issue that has been only very partially addressed. Here are examples of the measures that could be part of a vigorous global effort:

- Global satellite detection and remote sensing systems.

- International support efforts for countries that are repeatedly struck by disasters—such as Bangladesh—helping them with levees, dams, floodgates, land use planning, preparedness, emergency services, disaster management systems, alert systems. Even less-exposed countries need help in integrating disaster management into their development plans, given the increased incidence of freak catastrophes. This includes international sharing of experience in establishing and administering building codes and standards.

- Global efforts to promote microfinance and microinsurance approaches to both prevention and mitigation of risks, making them available to highly vulnerable poor people.

- An international setup for interconnecting emergency response and civil defense systems.

- Worldwide efforts to place insurance companies and capital markets more at the heart of the response system, for example, by promoting financial risk-sharing through "disaster bonds," which pay an extra-high yield but whose repayment of principal decreases for designated disasters, or through weather futures and other derivatives.

Natural disaster management provides one of the clearest illustrations of why some global issues are about sharing our humanity. These disasters have grown so in scope and frequency that, like all the issues in this chapter, they imply responsibilities for the global community. The next category is entirely different.

14
Sharing Our Rule Book: Issues Needing a Global Regulatory Approach

Most human affairs need no regulation, or need regulation only within nation-states. But for some areas, global regulation is needed to avoid leakages or free riders. These are areas where it's in the world's interest to have some rules, but where the rules will work only if all nation-states adopt them in common. Why? Because if only some countries adopt the rules, the activities they try to regulate will escape to noncomplying, free-rider countries. Worse, some countries could even make a business of noncompliance, causing leaks in the overall effort.

This third category of issues is much harder to write up and summarize in vivid terms, for two reasons: what you're trying to regulate is what's trying to hide or what hasn't really surfaced yet; and the regulation issues are often very complex. So for most, I'll give just a glimpse.

Reinventing Taxation for the Twenty-First Century

It is hard to see how the world will get by without a major global rethinking of taxation—and sooner rather than later. There are four main reasons for this.

First, the *new world economy*—with its rapid rate of change and its increasing reliance on virtual, delocalized processes—is creating huge challenges for the world's generally slow-moving, highly paper-based, and highly inflexible territorial tax systems. It's a real time bomb, and it affects corporate taxes, personal income taxes, sales taxes, and virtually all other forms of taxation:

- Corporate taxpayers have become more mobile and book more and more of their profits in lower-tax locations. Think of the example of Washington doctors dictating notes over the phone to typists in India: the company can book its profits either in India or in the United States. Many British gambling operations have recently set up on-line operations offshore. More broadly, with companies increasingly working through teams whose members are scattered across many countries, it becomes harder for any one country to claim the right to tax the results. No wonder some offshore tax havens have now started to also market themselves as e-commerce centers. To complicate things: with companies increasingly ready and able to relocate, you can bet that tax competition will increase—particularly when countries like Ireland have shown how successful low-tax policies can be in attracting corporations.

- Individual taxpayers can become more mobile and elusive as well. And this can have major consequences: in the United States, for instance, the top 1 percent of earners provide 30 percent of the personal income tax proceeds. The Internet makes it harder to pinpoint the identity and location of individuals engaged in taxable activities. And they can more readily move their taxation to lower-taxed places—with many more ways to do this than before, especially when it comes to capital income. All this means that richer, more mobile taxpayers start free-riding on the less mobile, less cosmopolitan taxpayers.

- E-commerce transactions are much harder for the taxman to track than traditional ones, particularly as the middlemen (who play an

> important role in tax collection and information) get cut out. Buy a book in New York, and you'll pay an 8.25-percent sales tax; order it from Amazon.com and you pay no tax at all. In Europe, a British firm selling on-line to a German client should apply the German value-added tax, but will the British authorities really feel responsible to check this out?

These problems—and there are others—will only worsen as the new world economy phenomenon deepens, particularly as e-commerce develops, with anonymous e-money in its wake (see below).[1] And this may come at a bad time, just as governments start having fiscal worries due to the aging of the population and the increasing burden of pension costs. On that account alone, a major global rethinking of taxation will have to take place.

But there's a second reason for such a rethinking, and it has to do with preserving the planet's *environment.* As we saw, the entirely different energy profile needed as part of the fight against global warming won't be achieved without powerful tax incentives. It is especially urgent that the world start thinking about a carbon tax to help it take a major turn towards higher energy efficiency and the decarbonization of the energy system through renewable energy and other means. More generally, given the magnitude of a whole range of environmental issues, the time will come when taxes on goods consumed will have to reflect their environmental cost through some sort of green or eco-taxes—if the world is really serious about these issues.

A third reason to rethink taxation has to do with its *goals and structure*. There are a variety of issues to think about. For instance, carbon and eco-taxes, needed as they are, imply an increase in the relative weight of indirect taxation (on what you consume) compared with direct taxation (on your income). Efforts to offset the greater elusiveness of incomes through more taxation at the consumption level may change this balance in the same direction. And some people claim that taxing consumption (defined as income less savings) is the way of the future, a proposal that also connects to another older idea, recently even alluded to by U.S. Secretary of the Treasury Paul O'Neill, of doing away with corporate taxation because it leads to income being taxed twice.

But the increased weight of indirect taxation that would result from all of these changes, badly needed as some may be, would be unfair to lower-income taxpayers—requiring in turn some thinking about negative income taxes (subsidies, in a way). As you can sense, rethinking taxation appears to be both a must and a mess, as it would raise unusually complex issues—and I have hardly scratched the surface of all the ideas that are around, such as the idea of a tax on speculative capital flows (the so-called Tobin tax) or on arms sales to catch two birds at once: slowing them by "throwing sand in the wheels" and raising funds for global causes.[2]

The fourth and final reason to rethink taxation relates to taxation *methods*. Two examples. The United States (along with the Philippines and Eritrea) taxes its nationals based on citizenship wherever they are; all other countries tax on the basis of residence. It's hard to see how the world's taxation systems can be streamlined with these two conflicting methods coexisting—and this messiness is bound to increase as more developing countries adopt the citizenship criterion in an effort to tax their skilled emigrants. A second question of method concerns automatic exchanges of tax information between jurisdictions.[3] Such exchanges will increasingly be on the agenda because they would kill three birds at once: turning harmful tax competition into healthy tax competition, helping identify possibly destabilizing capital flows, and tracing cross-border money laundering and terrorism finance flows (someone called this "throwing light on the wheels," rather than sand in the wheels).

Tax issues are sufficiently complex that *any* idea for changing taxation comes with strong pros and cons. But one thing is sure: the inevitable changes that will inevitably have to be made in the methods of taxation should not happen in some countries but not in others, if we are to avoid an unholy and unhealthy mess. The world would be far better with some sort global framework for rethinking taxation for the twenty-first century.[4] It would be best if this rethinking started very soon: the cat is already out of the bag, and the traditional, mostly territorial taxation approaches perfected in the twentieth century are poorly adapted to what is to come.

Biotechnology Rules

Biotechnology rules, not even a topic twenty years ago, have been made a pressing global issue by the spectacular explosion of discoveries in recent years. Yet biotechnology is still in its infancy, so far bringing up many more questions and possibilities than answers and outcomes. You can already sense, however, that this is an area where some sort of minimum critical mass of global rules will be needed—even if these rules aren't too clear yet.

Several areas come to mind. They all spring from the basic advances scientists have made in decrypting the basic code of life—DNA, RNA, and the proteins they trigger—in a revolution revealing that all living organisms are information-processing machines. But they have very different features. Here are three such areas:

- *Transgenic plants and animals.* Plant and animal breeding or hybridization to achieve desired features, a slow process, is very old. What's new is the direct manipulation of their genetics, which goes faster and much further. Farmers now plant some 50 million hectares a year with such genetically modified crops as soybeans, corn, cotton, and canola—98 percent in the United States, Canada, and Argentina, and the rest in more than ten countries. Three of every four hectares are devoted to crops engineered to withstand spraying of weed killers, the rest to crops modified to produce their own insecticides or to have some other feature. Some of these features could be very attractive: drought- and flood-resistant grass peas in Bangladesh are being modified so that they are no longer toxic when eaten in large amounts during famines; some plants are being modified to grow on lands with a high salt content. Transgenic plants, animals, and bacteria that produce raw materials (like plastics or tough silk proteins) and clean up polluted sites are beginning to be developed; some modified organisms could even feed on natural gas. Other genetically modified animals include salmon that grow faster and bigger.

- *Stem cell and other cloning applications.* As the undifferentiated cells from which other, more specialized cells arise, "stem cells" can be collected from embryos, fetuses, umbilical cords, or even adults, and—when given the right biochemical push—made to develop into various sorts of adult cell types. This technology, which can involve so-called therapeutic cloning, could be used to produce such things as virus-free blood supplies in unlimited quantities, dopamine-producing cells for Parkinson's sufferers, and made-to-measure cell replacements that won't be rejected by the patient. The variations around the theme are endless and awesome. Some applications, of the reproductive cloning variety, are straight out of a Frankenstein movie.[5]

- *Revolutionizing the treatment of diseases through detailed genome knowledge.* The deciphering at the very end of the last century of the human genome, with its 30,000 genes, turns out to be just a first step. Much of life's variety and complexity revolves not around DNA and RNA but around the mysterious interplay of the proteins they trigger. Yet the mere possibilities brought forth by genome knowledge are mind-blowing: more accurate diagnoses; drugs that work the first time and have no side effects; predictive medicine that can alert you ahead of time to what diseases you are at risk for; the ability to predict a virus's virulence from its genetic structure. Similar benefits of genome knowledge will accrue for domesticated animals as well.

Why would one need rules? For several reasons:

- *Moral reasons.* Some of the applications, such as those that involve the destruction of embryos for the embryonic variety of stem cells, clash with strongly held moral and religious principles. That conflict led the U.S. government in 2001 to severely limit research on them. Other governments feel equally queasy.

- *Threats to ecosystems and other species*. Like the hybrid varieties that have helped increase food supply as population grew, transgenic plants have a key role to play in helping the world feed itself in the decades to come. Yet they entail special risks: for instance, they could cross-pollinate with their wild relatives in highly damaging ways. Insect-resistant plants could wipe out important insects. Sexy-looking but sterile modified salmons could escape and thwart the reproduction of their wild brethren. People have even developed allergies to a modified variety of corn in late 2000—easily handled, but a warning.

- *Social risks*. Genome knowledge could create hitherto unknown and hard-to-manage tensions. People's genetic databases could show up in many places—voluntarily in medical databases, not-so-voluntarily in legal databases or even in private databases assembled outside their knowledge. Such databases could be abused to deny life or medical insurance, influence recruitment decisions, track real parenthood ties against people's wishes, or even create, as a British libertarian put it, a "nation of suspects."

Anyone who argues that no rules whatsoever are required is a fool. Even arguing that nation-state rules are sufficient is an uphill task: from the few examples and risks just listed, it is clear that this is an area where some minimal body of global rules, if only provisional ones, is a must. Cross-pollination and similar risks cannot be contained inside borders, and it is in everyone's interest that testing be done first, under safety conditions for which there is a global standard. Another reason for global action: what point is there in limiting embryonic stem cell research in the United States if there are no such rules elsewhere? Already, some U.S. companies are contemplating moving to the United Kingdom.[6] And what good is it for the United Kingdom or Sweden, say, to forbid involuntary inclusions of people's genetic data in private databases, when these databases may be available in cyber-space or you can send a skin flake to have a test done across the border?

Global Financial Architecture

This complex issue has many subparts. Simplifying a bit, four main areas require stepped-up global problem-solving: managing international financial crises, strengthening financial systems at large, dealing with financial abuse, and preparing for the future consequences of e-money. Despite progress on the first three, particularly in the last three years, none of the four has been addressed in a convincing, reassuring way.

MANAGING INTERNATIONAL FINANCIAL CRISES. What looked like a manageable problem in Thailand in August 1997 flared up into a two-year, continents-spanning financial crisis in the emerging markets of East Asia, and then even in Russia and Brazil. In late 1998, it threatened even broader damage. Seasoned observers were stunned by the speed and many channels of the contagion—capital flight, banks withdrawing their funds, declining commodity prices, abrupt and indiscriminate portfolio readjustments away from emerging markets, highly leveraged hedge funds suddenly reversing gears. The crisis inflicted a lot of damage, particularly in Indonesia, Thailand, Korea, the Philippines, and Malaysia; poor people were affected the most.

In 1997–1998, the IMF and others organized large rescue or "bailout" packages to help affected countries—the 1998 Korean package alone came to $57 billion. Those rescue packages, like that for Mexico a few years before, became the target of much criticism and debate. Many argued, for example, that the promise of such bailouts created incentives for private investors to take reckless risks once again in the future—the moral hazard problem.

Even today, there are wide-ranging views on how best to respond when such a crisis hits countries. There are two approaches in principle. One is to have lenders of last resort, like the IMF, put together large rescue packages to help crisis-affected countries for as long as the crisis lasts. The other is to allow these countries to temporarily stop payments on their debts and then renegotiate them. Despite much debate over the last four years, each of these options carries major unanswered questions:

- The rich countries, and the new U.S. administration, have become even more reluctant to pour vast amounts of money into bail-outs. The rescue packages for Turkey and Argentina in 2001 were preceded by continued and nagging uncertainty over what the accepted principles of such packages are.[7]

- For a while, the rich countries thought the way forward was to put crisis lending on a more systematic footing by promoting a contingent credit line window at the IMF. Countries would prequalify for support and would signal private investors how much help they could draw on. But the window remains essentially unused.

- Some thought the best way would be to expose weaknesses in countries' financial systems early, but a true crisis alert system managed by the IMF would place that institution in a position where it could itself end up triggering panics.

- If there's little enthusiasm for multibillion-dollar bailouts, there has been even less progress on the other theoretical option—the one under which countries would be allowed to temporarily stop payment while they negotiate a reduction in debt. Related to this, the broader idea of "bailing in" private lenders and investors in a crisis—to oblige them to participate in the pain of crisis resolution—hasn't gotten much further than very general debate. Most plans for formally roping in these players had run out of steam by mid–2000. There is, in short, still no equivalent for countries of the U.S. Chapter 11 rules that enable struggling debtors to temporarily suspend their payments—in spite of recent signs of greater enthusiasm for the idea on the part of some key U.S., European, and IMF officials, in the wake of the recent Argentina default.[8]

There have been hundreds of debates, proposals, and committees since 1997—even a special G20 effort that I will discuss in Part Three. But one still cannot say, after several years of discussion and continued crises, that there is any structured, well-known set of rules and mechanisms for financial crisis management. The main principle that seems to have emerged is the case-by-case approach. Undeniably, there has been progress in some areas, but overall, as economist Joseph Stiglitz mused two years ago, "a mountain gave birth to a mouse." A report by former central bankers and finance ministers from emerging countries and another one commissioned by the Commonwealth Secretariat, both released in the fall of 2001, similarly underline the insufficient progress over the last three years.[9]

STRENGTHENING DOMESTIC FINANCIAL SETUPS. Worldwide, there have been more than 100 financial crises in the last forty years. Quite a few occurred in rich countries, like the United States, Spain, Sweden, and now Japan, to mention some spectacular ones. The cost of such crises, which in some countries are recurrent episodes, can be staggering: up to 40 percent of GDP in some developing countries, and even a remarkable 5 percent of GDP for the U.S. savings-and-loans crisis. Banking weaknesses have sometimes been the trigger for international contagion crises such as the one that broke out in Asia in 1997–1998, and even when they weren't, they have always acted to amplify such crises. In that sense, strengthening domestic financial systems is also a global issue.[10]

Yet here again, much remains to be done. Despite massive efforts by the IMF and the World Bank, too many countries still suffer from an accumulation of bad loans in the banking sector, weak banking supervision, weak corporate governance, and insufficiently developed securities markets (which, if they were more developed, would provide a healthy counterweight to the accident-prone banking sectors). In fact, the job of strengthening domestic financial sectors is so great—and countries are often so reluctant to let others peek into their banking sectors—that this remains an area ripe for a massive global drive to get the job done across some 100 countries, based on globally shared principles.[11]

Part of that global action has to go beyond strengthening financial sectors within each individual country. There are some global, systemic issues that need to be tackled as well. Four examples:

- Worldwide rules on minimum risk capital for banks are in a state of flux. An older "capital ratio" formula has now been phased out by a committee managed by the Bank for International Settlements (BIS) and is about to be replaced by a new setup that takes hundreds of pages to describe—raising quite a few controversies. There is still some unfinished business there.

- Accounting rules for financial institutions remain oddly unclear in some major respects. One reason banking sectors are so opaque and able to hide serious problems for so long is that loans remain booked at their historical value. Serious accounting would imply, instead, that bankers constantly revalue their loans based on what has happened to interest rates or to the credit of borrowers. Tricky as it is, this "marking-to-market" is feasible—Danish banks do it. And oddly, the principle has been applied to the so-called swaps (derivative financial transactions through which two players exchange obligations), creating a real mess because loans aren't so treated.[12] At any rate, much work remains to be done on the accounting underpinnings of sound banking.

- Hedge funds remain poorly known and monitored financial creatures. The Long-Term Capital Management debacle in late 1998 (Chapter 7) brought hedge funds into the public limelight, and they have never left it since. Hedge funds are private funds that borrow up to fifteen to thirty times their own resources and then further leverage up to often gigantic positions through futures, options, and other derivatives—tools enabling sophisticated bets on the prices or price differences of other assets. Long-Term Capital Management, with equity capital of less than $5 billion, had at times more than $1 trillion in derivatives exposure. These hedge funds are mostly in the business of chasing tiny pricing aberrations between pairs of financial assets, which they then exploit at the large scale made possible by their large leverage. But sometimes their positions are more like huge outright bets on the possible rise or fall of a financial asset's price. In 1997, one hedge fund held positions on the Thai baht amounting to 20 percent of the Thai central bank's reserves. An intriguing recent casualty was the U.S. energy company Enron, which turned out to have a large hedge fund operation inside its belly when it collapsed in December 2001. Worldwide, there are now some 6,000 to 7,000 hedge funds controlling assets worth $500 billion, not including less visible ones like in the Enron case.[13] There is some work going on to develop some principles for stronger monitoring by governments of hedge funds and their potentially destabilizing activities, but it's still early days.

- Recent cases of sudden corporate collapse (Enron, Global Crossing, and several others within and outside the United States) have revealed major weaknesses in the world's accounting and auditing setups for corporations. In some of these cases, proceeds from borrowings were made to look like operating cash flow, debts were hidden in special vehicles, a range of exceptional items was omitted from the bottom line, and auditors were allowed to get away with serious conflicts of interest. The resulting credibility crisis has also highlighted how badly the world needs a unified set of principles for financial reporting, unlike today's different national approaches. For example, the U.S. accounting and financial reporting method is based on a very large number of detailed rules. This can encourage companies to comply with the letter of the law rather than its spirit. By contrast, some countries like the United Kingdom apply broader, more subjective principles that give more emphasis to the economic substance of companies' activities than to detailed rules; companies must, for instance, publish details of any subsidiary over which they have a significant influence. It would be far more sensible to have a global set of principles shared by all countries, based on worldwide best practices.

MONEY LAUNDERING AND OTHER FINANCIAL ABUSES. The amount of dirty or even downright dangerous money being cleaned through the world's financial system is huge—some $0.5 to $1.5 trillion a year, equivalent to 1.5 to 5 percent of the gross world product. Drug money, funds diverted by predatory rebel groups, government funds stolen by kleptocratic elites, flight capital and tax evasion proceeds of all kinds, and even terrorist networks' funds all mingle with legitimate funds in the world's enormous financial machinery. The parts of that machinery that wittingly or unwittingly facilitate money laundering are secrecy-promoting offshore banking centers; "shell" or "brassplate" banks that have no physical existence; and the "don't ask, don't tell" private banking practices followed to some extent everywhere. Even the world's giant mesh of correspondent banking links—through which money can be shifted in seconds between banks in different parts of the world that have accounts with each other but may not even be aware of each other's true nature—plays an unwitting part in this. As the world's biggest banks have up to 5,000–10,000 or more correspondent banking links, hiding or not seeing things becomes very easy.

A task force of twenty-nine leading countries and two international bodies, launched by the G7 in 1989 and managed by the Organization for Economic Cooperation and Development (OECD), called the Financial Action Task Force (FATF), has come up with forty criteria covering financial regulation, law enforcement, and international collaboration. Based on these criteria, it has exposed more than a dozen countries suspected of tolerating money laundering, from Russia and Israel to the Marshall Islands. Within a year, half of these countries were busy passing legislation to try to get themselves off the list—a remarkable "reputation effect" discussed later in the book. But a recent revised list had nineteen countries again, and more are likely to be added.

Yet the FATF list, even with its prominent targets, is far from the kind of global effort the world's money-laundering plague warrants. There are bigger problems to tackle across the whole family of nations. Just think of the correspondent banking system. In March 2001, no fewer than fifteen U.K. banks were found to have significant weaknesses in their money-laundering controls, letting $1.3 billion pass through accounts linked to the family of former Nigerian ruler Sani Abacha. Later that year, it was made known that the United States itself failed to comply with twenty-eight of the FATF's forty criteria. And clearly, as the events of September 11, 2001, showed, there has been a major worldwide failure to detect major terrorist actions from suspect money movements and to curb terrorism finance itself.

Terrorism finance presents a special challenge: it amounts to "reverse money laundering," as it takes legitimate-looking business or charitable funds and puts them into terrorist activities. It is therefore hard to track. There's no alternative to asking banks worldwide to carefully check the identity of depositors; getting bank supervisors to share information between jurisdictions and to allow for cross-border police searches of suspect accounts; and prohibiting secretive money-forwarding, like the so-called *hawala* system used by the terrorists.[14] And there's no way around beefing up the existing global framework for monitoring all of this: at the beginning of September 2001, the FATF Secretariat had fewer than ten staff.

Financial abuse thus connects to many other global scourges—from drug trafficking to terrorism financing to kleptocratic government. And it is an inherently global issue: cracking down on domestic banks within individual countries, if it isn't copied by jurisdictions elsewhere, may do little more than make those banks and countries uncompetitive in the new world economy. This is par excellence the free-rider and leakage theme that underlies so many issues in the third category.

PREPARING FOR E-MONEY. This part of the global financial architecture issue is more futuristic but no less important. Today, the control by central banks over interest rates rests on the fact that households and firms need money for transactions—and that banks can create money only if they hold enough reserves at the central bank. But over the next twenty years, the new world economy is likely to move further into the direction of electronic money—a private form of money that could reduce the role of orthodox money and thus of central banks. E-money could consist of prepaid smart cards, where money is stored on a computer chip, and of software-based payment systems run by private e-money issuers. Households and firms would then accept and swap balances in the books of these e-money issuers—reducing the part of the flow of money that goes through banks and hence through central bank control.

In such a world, people could choose which currency bloc they want to belong to, and there would be an increasing disconnect between territorial nation-states and the money used to settle physical transactions conducted on their territory.[15] The consequences for central banks' monetary policy and even their role as lenders of last resort would be tremendous. And this is not just a wild speculation: for several years, Singapore has been devising ways to replace cash and checks with electronic payments, in the hope of eliminating coins and bills by 2008.[16] Even if Singapore weren't to meet its deadline, the question is not whether e-money will happen, but when. Why? Because e-money is driven by a powerful logic that has to do with the elimination of the usual time lag between transactions and their final settlement—so a seller will no longer have to worry about the other party's creditworthiness. Eliminate that, and you eliminate much of the raison d'être for traditional money and banking intermediation, with all that rides on it, including the central bank's gatekeeping role.

You might therefore imagine that e-money is the subject of many in-depth global debates and preparations, but you would be wrong. In this "dog years" area, little global debate has occurred as yet—as with rethinking taxation.

With its four parts, the challenge of improving the global financial architecture amounts to an urgent global issue—unresolved, it leaves the new world economy with a serious weakness.[17] It also raises free-rider and leakage issues. And despite many efforts since the 1997–1998 financial crisis, it is far from having been definitively tackled.

Illegal Drugs

The world market for illegal drugs—some $150 billion retail, involving some 200 million users—is the world's largest illicit market. Some believe it may be even larger, up to $400 billion all included. It is a huge market even in relative terms: about half the size of the pharmaceuticals market, and close to the tobacco and alcohol markets of $200 billion or so each. Of the $150 billion total, the United States and Europe account for $60 billion each—the two largest markets by far. In the United States, the total population of users has stabilized somewhat since the crack cocaine, cocaine, and heroin peaks in the 1970s and 1980s—but heavy users seem to be using more drugs and harming themselves more. And in many rich countries other than the United States, such as the United Kingdom, the numbers of both casual and heavy users are still rising.

Drug use is also rising in Russia and Eastern Europe, Asia, and now even Africa: crack cocaine has spread quickly since 1995 in South Africa, which may have the worst drug problem in that continent. And one easily forgets that Pakistan, Thailand, China, and Iran still account for most of the world's heroin consumption. Drug trafficking now touches some 170 countries.

By contrast, production is concentrated in only a few countries. In 2000, about two-thirds of opium used for heroin production was from Afghanistan, and most of the remainder from Myanmar. Colombia accounts for two-thirds of cocaine production. Among synthetic drugs, the Netherlands and some Eastern European countries (Poland) are the world's main producers of ecstasy, while methamphetamines are produced mostly on the U.S.-Mexican border and in places like Myanmar. Only cannabis, being more bulky and less valuable, is grown a little bit everywhere, near its markets. But synthetic drugs can also be manufactured almost anywhere, presenting a new, rapidly spreading phenomenon.[18]

Like many other businesses, the illegal drug business has begun to reshape itself along the tenets of the new world economy, running more efficiently than ever—particularly when it comes to distribution. Colombian suppliers team up with Mexican smugglers with strong logistics skills. Small aircraft, global positioning systems, and cellular phones are put to systematic use; top managers with prestigious MBAs run the traffickers' finance and money-laundering operations. Ordinary businesses in Spain play a key role in bringing cocaine into Europe. Israeli crime syndicates handle a large chunk of the ecstasy trade between the Netherlands and the United States. Closely linked immigrant communities speaking languages that the police cannot understand do retail distribution: in Denmark, the Gambians; in Australia, the Vietnamese. Vastly more efficient distribution and shipping are among the major factors behind the recent halving of heroin and cocaine prices in the United States.

The illegal drug trade inflicts damage at several levels:

- In poor countries that produce the drugs, the revenues often fuel internal conflicts (see Chapter 13) and massive corruption in police, army, and government circles—the sort that can wreck a country's entire potential for development and poverty reduction. Some of these revenues can end up in the war chests of international terrorist groups, or even finance an entire rogue state. Worldwide, some $80–100 billion ends up channeled in such unsavory directions. Some of Afghanistan's revenues from the drug trade may have benefited the Al-Qaeda network.[19]

- In countries whose citizens consume the drugs, health is one of the main concerns. Heroin wrecks lives. Needle sharing spreads AIDS and hepatitis. Even cannabis can alter brain activity and, by some accounts, brings about higher incidences of car accidents. Yet few would disagree that the health damage from most drugs is far less than that inflicted by tobacco and alcohol consumption. Cannabis, for one, may be even less addictive and generally less of a health threat than those two. And apart from heroin, few people die from drug use.

- In consuming countries, the bigger damage is from the criminal activity around the drug trade—from the shoplifting, burglaries, and prostitution that so-called chaotic users resort to, and from the vicious circle of marginalization of the generally poor communities that end up suffering most from the trade. About 30 percent of crimes leading to arrests in the United Kingdom had as their motive the need to find money for crack or cocaine. In the United

> States, drug use is 50 percent more common in households on welfare. Almost all drug-related arrests in the United States are from the bottom of the drug-dealing pyramid, and three-fourths of those arrested are from non-white, impoverished communities—all part of the process that puts more young black men in the United States in prison than in college.

How successful have current antidrug policies been worldwide? While very expensive, these policies have often yielded little in the way of lasting results because they focus almost exclusively on the supply side. The most extensive antidrug policy is in the United States. It costs some $30 billion per year in cash, about half of the total retail market size of $60 billion. Of this, three-fourths is spent on the supply side combating the production and distribution of drugs—from faraway countries to the streets and backrooms where they are sold to users.

Unfortunately, these kinds of policies have revealed serious limitations:

- Without a forceful global coalition, the effort to combat the production of drugs in the exporting countries has often resulted in mere relocation and reorganization of production rather than an overall cutback. Dramatic falls in coca production in Peru and Bolivia in the 1990s, for example, simply brought increased production in Colombia. Drugs are just too profitable, and production is cheap and moveable.

- Shipping is also so profitable that cutting it off in one place results in its resurfacing elsewhere. A pilot demanding $500,000 to fly 250 kilograms of cocaine adds only 2 percent to the street price of $100,000 per kilogram; if the plane later has to be abandoned, the cost merely doubles to 4 percent. And shipping can deftly pick new routes: Africa has lately become an active trans-shipping platform for drugs destined to Europe from Asia and Latin America. The profitable drug trade also makes it easy to entice police and customs officials on both sides of the shipment to close their eyes.

- Cutting off distribution is even harder. Some 100 groups bring cocaine into the United States; cut off one, another takes over. Among all arrests made in the United States for drug offenses, 40 percent are only for possessing cannabis, while fewer than 20 percent are for the sale or manufacture of drugs, whether heroin, cocaine, or anything else. Unlike other crimes, the seller and the buyer agree and there's no complaining witness, so police must rely on clumsy informant, wiretap, and undercover tactics—with the risk of harming civil liberties in the process.

What's the way out? There has been some new thinking, much of it quite controversial. It goes roughly like this: much of the damage inflicted by the drug trade throughout the world—as well as the difficulty of cutting off the very profitable production, shipping, and distribution activities—has to do with the massive price wedge between the import and retail prices of illegal drugs. Example: in late 2000, a kilogram of opium would get $90 for a Pakistani or Afghan farmer, a kilogram of heroin (requiring 10 kilograms of opium) would wholesale locally for $3,000, then be resold for $80,000 in the United States and retail for $290,000 per kilogram on the streets.

This price wedge, so the argument continues, ends up benefiting rogue states, terrorism, criminality, corruption—and leads to the marginalization of poor communities and individuals caught up in the drug system. And it's the price wedge that makes cutting off the trade so difficult and often futile. Yet, paradoxically, the price wedge is the direct result of the rich countries' strenuous efforts to cut off the supply.

This type of reasoning has led quite a few people and even governments to conclude that a global solution may have to entail a concerted reduction of the price wedge. How? By focusing policy, they suggest, less on supply and more on the demand side. Practically, this would have two aspects:

- First, it would mean selectively liberalizing the laws regarding possession and trade of at least the less addictive illegal drugs. The aim would be to drive down the profitability of a big chunk of the drug trafficking business; to keep users of softer drugs away from dealers in harder drugs; and to reduce the marginalization of drug users. Even the United Kingdom has recently moved into that direction, while avoiding outright legalization. Backers of this idea bring up studies showing that tobacco leads the league table when it comes to addiction (80 percent of smokers are addicted) against recovery rates of 40–50 percent for heroin and 90 percent for cocaine, while cannabis and amphetamines may not be psychologically addictive. They also bring up evidence showing that the "gateway theory" whereby soft drugs lead onto the path of hard drugs has little basis in fact.

- Second, so the new thinking proponents say, it would mean treating drug addiction more as a public health and social marginalization problem than as a local drug criminality problem. In Switzerland, researchers are beginning to find that even for highly addictive drugs like heroin, publicly managed, carefully monitored "heroin maintenance" programs have better results for addicts than expensive and often futile detoxification programs, or even heroin-substitute programs such as methadone maintenance. In France, there are innovative efforts to do something about the high-school dropouts from poor communities who so easily become the foot soldiers of drug distribution and related criminal activities. The Écoles de la Seconde Chance, run in partnership with businesses, provide dropouts with an intensive catch-up program aimed at developing a particular skill; this approach works and is cost-effective from a public resource standpoint.[20]

What's global in all this? Since it touches more than 170 countries, illegal drug trafficking is certainly a global issue. Yet despite quite a few conventions and international efforts, it's hard not to conclude that the world's been on a treadmill in this area. Three reasons argue for urgent global action.

First, the new thinking just described—reducing the price wedge, focusing resources and policies less on supply and more on the demand side, zeroing in more on public health and social marginalization aspects—while certainly not uncontroversial (if only because its proponents aren't very crisp about the risk that drug consumption could increase with lower prices)—looks to some governments as an end to decades of disappointing results from traditional policies. Some of these governments, particularly in Europe, have been moving in that direction and have shown good results, for example, in reduced criminality. But these experiments, particularly in the Netherlands and Switzerland, have also shown that any country that moves way ahead of others turns into a net exporter. Putting it another way: the policies of the world's biggest importers, like the United States, will limit the freedom of other countries to move towards the potentially more promising new thinking.

So there's a strong reason for urgent thinking and action in a concerted, global format—all countries have to move roughly in sync, or it's better to leave the new thinking alone. What's more, *if* the world concluded that the new thinking should be given a chance, then the shelter of some sort of global framework will also be required, or else national politicians who would embrace some of the new thinking will readily be branded by their opponents as in favor of drug taking—a sure way to halt the process.

The second reason to consider urgent global action has to do with production. Stopping the production of heroin or cocaine may be hard, but it's less hard than trying to cut off shipping or distribution, in part because the production is more concentrated geographically. There have been many efforts to do this, sometimes international efforts, sometimes special efforts by one country like the United States in Colombia. But there has not been a massive, concerted global drive. Nor has there been a large enough companion drive to help countries develop large-scale alternatives to opium or coca growing. There is a compelling reason to think of such an effort now, even in the framework of the new thinking above, with its lesser emphasis on supply cutoff. And that is the glaring link between these production activities and issues like terrorism financing, money laundering, and rogue state financing. This goes beyond antidrug concerns and connects to other global issues. The events of fall 2001 made very clear the urgency of helping Afghanistan replace poppy growing with something else, and this was indeed discussed with its provisional authorities as early as December 2001. The same applies to quite a few other countries.

The third reason has to do with the worrisome ascent of a whole array of synthetic drugs. They pose a novel problem to the world, possibly even a tougher one than traditional plant-based drugs. Often based on legal precursor products, they escape the traditional drug-control systems. And their innocuous appearance often leads users to underestimate their danger. Serious thinking about what to do globally in precursor control, information, and early warning when new products burst into a market has only begun. This subissue has all the makings of another massive challenge altogether—and had better be tackled globally and early.

Trade, Investment, and Competition Rules

This global issue is a cause célèbre, if only because protest movements have chosen to concentrate on it so much more than on the other nineteen or so. It comprises one urgent issue, trade rules, and two slightly less urgent ones, global investment and competition rules. Some people like to jumble them all up, but that just adds to the confusion.

Trade Rules. The story is simple. Shortly after World War II, the rich countries started freeing trade and reducing tariffs, mostly through the General Agreement on Tariffs and Trade (GATT). The results were stunning: between 1950 and 2000, world output was multiplied by five, world merchandise exports by eighteen.

Developing countries were little involved in these efforts until the 1980s, when they started opening their economies to trade as part of the economic revolution that has acted as one of the two engines of the new world economy (Chapter 3). For them the results were also extraordinary: for instance, over just the last decade, they lifted their share of merchandise exports (other than oil) from 18 percent of the world total to 25 percent. Lately, they have been doing well even in services exports—recall the performance of India's Bangalore in software exports and other examples (Chapter 4). Developing countries now account for one-fourth of total trade in services.

This has been one major factor behind the 3.5-percent average economic growth of the developing countries in the 1990s, exceeding that of the rich countries. And those that opened their economies the most—including Mexico, Brazil, China, India, Malaysia, Bangladesh, Vietnam, Hungary, and even a few African countries—did the best both in economic growth and poverty reduction. A group of twenty-four such "globalizers" from the developing world—with 3 billion people—increased their per capita income by about 5 percent a year during the 1990s, against a 1-percent decline for the other developing countries—with 2 billion people—that did the least to integrate themselves in the new world economy.[21] Many countries in the latter group are part of the group of fifty-odd "least developed countries," which even saw its share of world exports move down from 3 percent in the 1950s to less than 1 percent today. These days, economic isolation is a fast track to impoverishment—and to diseases, degradation, and the despair that leads people to lose faith in their institutions.[22]

Further liberalization of trade should be a no-brainer. Indeed, studies show that a further substantial lowering of trade tariffs and barriers could lift world output by several hundred billion dollars a year, netting developing countries at least $50–100 billion a year in additional resources—resources that, as we saw, are badly needed to seriously reduce poverty on the planet.

But the story isn't simple after all. There have been massive complications and controversies around the attempt to move in such a direction by the more than 140 member states assembled in the World Trade Organization (WTO)—the global successor, created in January 1995, of the more secretive, rich country-oriented GATT. These complications, which predated the highly publicized Seattle fiasco of November 1999, are all the more intriguing as the WTO's membership has been steadily increasing—with the recent entry of China and Taiwan adding, in one fell swoop, 20 percent to the reach of trade liberalization.[23] But they are likely to become even more vividly clear as all the WTO members enter a three-year negotiation phase now that the November 2001 Doha meeting has managed to launch a new trade round, with a clear developing country-focused agenda.

If trade liberalization is so beneficial, and if the next round is indeed going to focus on the development agenda, where do these complications come from? Summarizing a bit, there are three major sources.

To start with, even though most developing countries have done nicely, emerging asymmetries have made many of them fear that rich countries will get disproportionately more out of future liberalization than they do. For one, many of them feel that they don't even have the resources and capacity to implement earlier agreements, such as the so-called Uruguay Round of 1994, which liberalized telecommunications and services, among others. What's more, they point out that greater market access will work only if they get help in addressing "behind-the-border" issues like their deficient ports, road networks, infrastructure, customs systems, quality certification setups, and sanitary controls. And finally, they feel that some new rules, such as those on intellectual property rights, may make them lose out to the rich countries in the increasingly knowledge-intensive new world economy. All these points have such validity that they do indeed form an urgent agenda for global action. Much needs to be done: despite scores of practical proposals by the developing countries in those directions over the last two years, there has been little action so far, leaving them quite disappointed.

The second big complication has to do with agricultural exports. Almost all developing countries—especially the lower-income ones and those in the "least developed countries" group—depend heavily on agricultural exports. For many of them, it's the only avenue towards lifting themselves and their people out of poverty. Yet the rich countries have not only failed to seriously reduce agricultural tariffs and barriers, but they continue subsidizing their own agriculture to the tune of $1 billion a day, depressing world prices and depriving poor countries of the chance to compete. In Europe alone, such subsidies cost every man, woman, and child nearly $200 a year. Subsidies also continue in Japan and in many other places, and have lately even increased in the United States.[24]

Reducing, let alone eliminating these subsidies is a political hot potato, even though the farmer population in the rich countries is an extremely small part of the electorate. For those who read between the lines, *this* may have been the major cause behind the debacle of the Seattle WTO meeting in the fall of 1999. It's not an issue that will go away—it's too central to solving the issue of poverty. But the contrived, tortured text of the Doha declaration that deals with this issue strongly hints that some rich countries will be very slow to address it.[25]

The third big complication has to do with manufactured exports from the developing world. Even though agricultural exports are a key agenda item for them, their manufactured exports have been growing nicely, with especially good prospects for growth in light, labor-intensive exports like textiles. Unfulfilled rich-country promises in the textile area, and rich country abuse of anti-dumping procedures, have been among the reasons for many developing countries' recent hard feelings.

But the issue is broader and deeper: it has to with a great anguish in many rich countries. Many rich-country politicians, union leaders, and others fear that if the developing countries are given greater access to their manufactured export markets, their often lower labor and environmental standards will help them outcompete and hurt rich-country producers, possibly even leading to a "race to the bottom." Note that there is no evidence whatsoever that as they lift their trade and growth performance, developing countries actively lower their standards, let alone become "pollution havens." Still, this second political hot potato is what led the United States and the EU to try to link labor and environmental issues to trade issues in Seattle—the second major reason for the debacle and for the uproar by the developing countries. Why did this proposal make developing countries so upset? Because most of them believe that trade sanctions applied for such reasons would be used to keep their products out—and that rich countries, as they often do, would pressure small countries more than big ones.

Those are the main complications around the very complex agenda of the international trade rules. Don't let their technical complexity and difficulty distract you from the huge stakes involved, the main one being poverty reduction. The proof will be in the pudding, particularly as far as agricultural subsidies are concerned.

At any rate, these complications explain why the malaise about global problem-solving seems to have somehow crystallized around this issue. And trade isn't alone. It has two companion issues.

INVESTMENT RULES. While the world makes a lot of noise around trade rules, another phenomenon has quietly begun to dominate the greater integration into the new world economy: foreign investment. It has soared even faster than trade over the last decades—about three times faster. Between 1980 and 2000, the total amount of foreign investment went from 4 percent to 12 percent of GDP as a worldwide average, but it surged even faster in developing countries, from 4 percent to 16 percent of their GDP.

There are now 63,000 multinational companies with 800,000 foreign affiliates. Those affiliates had sales of $11 trillion worldwide in 2000, a much higher figure than total world exports of $7 trillion. A Japanese or German car will often have been assembled in the United States from mostly U.S. components. To put it another way: foreign investment, which now runs at about $1 trillion a year (one-third in developing countries, two-thirds in rich countries) is the main vehicle for the buildup of the global production system that is at the heart of the new world economy (Chapters 3 and 4). It is rapidly emerging as more important in delivering goods and services to foreign markets than trade itself.

Yet unlike the global trade rules that the WTO administers, there are few international investment rules—instead, there have been many bilateral investment treaties (or "bits") between pairs of countries, with the EU as their main promoter. Their number has grown from some 400 in 1980 to close to 2,000 today, involving more than 170 countries.[26] This alone (but there are also other reasons) makes investment rules a global issue that needs tackling at some point, and better sooner than later: the enormous proliferation of "bits" confuses investors and leaves developing countries probably at a disadvantage on the whole. Yet it is seen as a perhaps less urgent issue than the trade issue, as shown by the many voices that have been objected to its inclusion in the already overly complicated trade rules negotiations to come.

COMPETITION RULES. This is a latecomer. Mergers reached more than $3 trillion worldwide in 1999, another sign of the massive restructuring of global production outside the domain of world trade. Those mergers do not raise global issues of their own, save for the problem that is created by the sheer number of countries (some sixty) in which these mergers must jump regulatory hurdles under national competition (antitrust) laws. When Alcan tried in late 2000 to achieve a deal with Pechiney and Alusuisse—which ended up unconsummated—the company had to file for approval in sixteen countries and in eight languages, with 400 boxes of documents and 1 million pages of e-mail.[27]

This and other questions are likely to make this an emerging global issue next to international trade and investment rules. Should one look for greater convergence among national antitrust definitions, regulations, and tests? How should national antitrust authorities deal with a corporate world whose real or virtual business now extends well beyond its territorial jurisdiction? How should they deal with the monopolies that can arise so quickly in some high-technology areas?

Summing up, the triple global issue of international trade, investment, and competition rules demands determined global action. The toughest challenge has to do with rethinking the rich world's enormous agricultural subsidies—and with cutting through the other obstacles and complications that have arisen around the expanded trade agenda. The urgency is all too clear: it has to do with giving the developing countries serious chances to achieve over the next decades the 5–6 percent annual growth rates needed to solve the biggest global issue of them all—poverty.

Intellectual Property Rights

The protection of intellectual property rights (IPRs)—patents, trademarks, copyrights, trade secrets, and the like—has changed over the last two decades from an obscure national regulation issue to a hotly debated global issue. It's a very complex issue to summarize, as there are quite a few strands. But behind all these strands, there is one central new world economy phenomenon.

The new world economy is, as we saw in earlier chapters, bent on knowledge and constant innovation—the opposite of a static economy. And here's the rub: in a static economy, there would be a case for giving intellectual property less protection than physical property. How so? Simply because an object used by X cannot be simultaneously used by Y, so that physical property rights are needed to avoid a war of all against all. By contrast, if X listens to a song or watches a film, Y can still do the same at near-zero additional cost, so that assigning property rights to them would merely result in the wasteful exclusion of would-be consumers.

But in the anything-but-static new world economy, just as physical property rights must be protected, some sort of protection of intellectual property rights is needed if there's going to be any incentive for people to try to invent new software, pharmaceutical drugs, songs, films, and so on. You could even argue that this protection is needed more than ever, as the cost of producing such innovations can be very heavy—some drugs costs several billion dollars to develop, some movies cost fortunes, some trademarks take decades to build into vouchers of quality. These costs are going up just as the new technologies make duplication and free dissemination easier than ever. The tension between the two is at its maximum in the new world economy.[28]

This explains why there are so many different strands to this issue and why the whole field is in such flux. Here's a triple sample:

- *Software*. The world is moving steadily in the direction of protecting software with patents, with the United States and Japan ahead of the rest of the world in this. Yet opponents argue that software should be no more patentable than a mathematical formula—and that protecting it will decrease innovation in that industry.[29] As an example of how big the stakes of the debate are, some upstart companies, like Ximian, have been trying to rewrite the rules of the software business by creating and giving away word processors, spreadsheets, e-mail readers and other programs that mimic the look and feel of Microsoft's signature products—yet Microsoft's $25 billion a year business is based on the idea that software should be owned and that its basic ingredients are proprietary.[30] Opponents also argue that strengthening software patenting could create monopolies for first movers—pointing to a tricky intersection between the promotion of competition (the role of antitrust laws) and the promotion of innovation (the role of intellectual property laws, whose aim is to protect innovators from competition long enough to make it worth their while to create in the first place).[31]

- *Biotechnology.* Patents are being issued for living organisms. This raises a host of issues: moral and religious issues for some people, perceived environmental risks (see above in this chapter), and worries by the developing countries that large multinationals will come to dominate the supply of seeds for new plant varieties. Some 920 patents have been taken out on rice, maize, soybean, wheat, and sorghum, 70 percent of them by six multinational companies.[32] This practice raises two worries: that more and more patents are being won for varieties where there is little evidence of innovation; and that farmers using patented crops will be forced into a royalty-paying system under which they are denied the right to save, grow, exchange, and resell seeds as they like. Another issue has become pressing as well: the patenting of decrypted gene sequences, which can raise delicate controversies. Human Genome Sciences is involved in one: having had the foresight to apply for a patent for the gene for CCR5, which, as a receptor, looked like a promising target for anti-AIDS drugs, it could now insist on cross-licensing by any other lab that would want to aim drugs at this receptor.[33]

- *Looming clash between developed and developing countries.* Many of the new IPR rules have been piggybacked onto the WTO even though they have only indirect links to international trade, as hinted by the title of the relevant agreement, the Agreement on Trade-Related Aspects of Intellectual Property Rights, or TRIPs—

quite a mouthful. For the developing world, most of these rules will kick in only around 2005, but the anguish is mounting, as the developing countries will have to remedy several typical weaknesses in their intellectual property systems: weak standards and limited enforcement of patents; lax or nonexistent copyright, trademark, and trade secret protection; and their frequent refusal to recognize patents on things like pharmaceutical products, agricultural chemicals, biotechnology, and new plants. Many developing countries see it this way: while the world at large will benefit from better incentives for innovation and creation, the developing country group will see its ability to imitate foreign products and technologies reduced. And they are afraid of a double cost burden: beside the massive expense of improving their own IPR administration systems, they may face higher prices for the protected products. This issue recently flared up in relation to the pricing and licensing of anti-AIDS drugs; how real it is for poor countries became clear when even the United States and Canada choked on the price of anthrax-fighting drugs and threatened for a short while to override patent rights in view of the bioterrorism menace.[34]

These three strands should give a sense of the urgency of moving to global solutions for this complex issue of IPRs. It is too central and too complex to be left under diverging national laws (outside the EU, no two countries so far have identical IPR laws). It is too important to be dealt with as a mere subpart of the largely unrelated and already difficult international trade negotiations. And it's an urgent issue at that—as reality has been moving much faster than the world's IPR setup for it. This is also true of the next issue.

E-Commerce Rules

These days, there are two ways to picture e-commerce. One is to think of the recent troubles of the dot-coms, many of which soared and crashed around e-commerce, and to see it as a smallish analog of catalogue sales, of particular use for business-to-business transactions—but not going very far. The other picture goes like this. Imagine 1 billion connected computers worldwide, in a not too distant future. Look at them as forming not just an on-line community but a "seventh continent"—a virtual continent with no time zones and no borders, with business transacted twenty-four hours a day, seven days a week, with passports reflecting not the place where you were born as much as your PC and Internet connection.[35]

The second view is more realistic. From a few billion dollars in the mid–1990s, e-commerce soared to $250 billion in 2001, and many forecasts put it above $3 trillion by 2005 or so. Some predict that by 2010, e-commerce could account for 15–20 percent of retail sales. If you believe that's too much, just remember that old-fashioned catalogue sales alone account for 10 percent of retail sales in the United States. But where e-commerce has so far been most successful is not in retail, business-to-customer sales but in the business-to-business area, which accounts for 80 percent of total e-commerce today. The scope for expansion remains very large, particularly as e-commerce picks up growth outside the United States, which has so far accounted for 70 percent of it.

Why this bullishness? Because for all its teething problems, e-commerce is driven by some enormous advantages that are bound to make it a huge phenomenon in the future:

- E-commerce has a global reach—no limits of shelf space or warehousing—so it can easily outdo the real world.
- Choice is greater, and prices are easily compared—recall the "nude economy" of Chapter 5.
- The costs of concluding and processing transactions are significantly lower.
- Transportation can be bulked or directed to the closest warehouse.

And if that isn't enough, e-commerce aggregates players worldwide—eBay, for example, brings together bidders from around the world, completely outdoing the local flea market.[36] What's more, e-commerce easily weaves in information of direct relevance to the customer's choice, as with Amazon.com's automatic suggestions of *other* books similar to the one you're looking at, and as with those e-commerce services that include the intervention of call centers. In the business-to-business area, e-commerce enables close cooperation between a firm, other firms, suppliers, and even customers—making everyone better off and smarter in the process (Chapter 4).

But coming with this likely future success is an urgent global issue in the making. There is a risk that e-commerce, along with its e-contracting and e-money cousins, will soar ahead of the world's ability to come up with at least a minimum number of global rules for it. Here are a few examples of problems that need to be addressed fast, through some sort of global approach:

- *Taxation.* This issue, discussed earlier, is complex and serious.

- *The impending logjam of national laws.* E-commerce brings forth an almost constant clash between the borderlessness of the "seventh continent" and the territoriality of nation-state laws (part of a more general clash alluded to in Chapter 7). People from anywhere buy from, and interact with, people from anywhere on the Internet. Yet Denmark bans advertising for children, France advertising in English, Germany comparative advertising. In a famous case, Yahoo! was sued in France for hosting web sites displaying and selling Nazi memorabilia—only to have a U.S. federal judge rule that Yahoo! could ignore the French court order.[37]

- *Adjudication of disputes*. Some countries, like those in the EU, feel that customers should be able to choose their home jurisdiction in case of disputes over an on-line transaction, rather than the home jurisdiction of the supplier, who can be anywhere. Other countries disagree. There are two ways to address these types of logjams.

Technical solutions, like filtering and "IP address" tracking of users, could help nation-states enforce their rules, but remain problematic.[38] And then there's the more or less unpalatable holy grail of e-commerce: a system (which does not, and may never exist) in which users would have permanent digital identities containing details of age, sex, citizenship, tax residency, professional credentials—something that would help nation-states reclaim ground even more systematically.[39] Failing to find acceptable technical solutions, nations would soon have to sit together and try to clear the logjam by unifying their laws—in such areas as advertising, hosting or jurisdictional disputes.

- *Building trust and confidence in e-commerce.* Nations would also do well to join forces early on a flurry of issues like electronic signatures and authentication, rules for electronic record keeping, rules on what constitutes consent, electronic copyright rules, basic principles of consumer protection in e-commerce, and, very important, rules for data privacy, data transfers, and encryption. Since e-commerce is still in its early days, it would really pay off to get countries to come together around the formulation of such rules. If this does not happen, expect a further logjam: just in the United States, for example, some forty states have independently adopted their own electronic signature rules. Extrapolate this to the world's 190 or so nation-states, and life on the seventh continent could become really complicated.

- *Protecting people, businesses, and societies from cyber-crimes.* Spreading Internet-related problems—such as hacking, credit card frauds, and viruses—are likely to set e-commerce back unless they are tackled through determined and early global action. This is an area where the potential for making nasty uses of technology has been way ahead of the ability of nations to protect their citizens.[40] Particularly worrisome are cryptography, where unbreakable systems have been commercialized without any "backdoor" for government security services—and steganography, which enables data, messages, and pictures to be hidden within normal-looking Internet pictures in ways that are almost impossible to detect. (It looks like some Al-Qaeda operatives may have used this technique.)[41]

It is hard to do justice to the variety and complexity of e-commerce issues in so little space. The main point is the urgency of solving this emerging global issue fast—while it is still in its infancy. There have been attempts, but they have occurred at the level of less-than-global groupings—from the OECD to the less well-known Council of Europe (with its forty member states) to some smaller regional groupings. All the while, national legislators continue to produce a dense thicket of often conflicting territorial laws on subjects that aren't well understood.

International Labor and Migration Rules

Here's an issue right at the confluence of the two big forces discussed in Part One. The new world economy force demands more attention to the labor rules national economies apply—as they interact more and more with each other. The demographic force throws in a series of migration-related issues. It is hard to imagine the world twenty years from now not having some sort of global labor market rules in place—because such a market is clearly in the making.

The issues around *labor rules* are both ancient and in flux. Ancient because one of the world's oldest international institutions, the International Labor Organization (ILO) has been at it since 1919. And in flux because things are changing so much, with new ways of working, more growth in independent work than in salaried work, and the decline of unions. Yet the greater interdependence between countries created by the new world economy makes it more urgent to find a stronger and broader global framework for labor rules than has evolved so far. Simplifying a bit, there are four levels to consider in such an effort:

- *Core labor rights*. Four preexisting "core labor standards" were reinforced by a 1998 declaration that many countries have adhered to:

prohibiting slave, bonded, and forced prison labor; prohibiting discrimination in the labor place for any reason; prohibiting child labor outside certain minimum age and other conditions, and combating its worst forms such as child prostitution, child sale and trafficking, child soldiers, and so on; and ensuring workers the freedom of association and collective bargaining. The main challenge is no longer the desirability or even definition of these standards, but worldwide enforcement.[42]

- *A broader set of labor rights*. For the twenty-first century, this could include health, safety, minimum working conditions, access to social safety nets, dispute resolution systems, and access to labor rights by nonsalaried workers, whose number is growing fast in the new world economy.

- *"Decent work."* There are new ideas around about moving beyond mostly negative labor rights (thou shall not use forced labor, and so on) towards emphasizing greater and more equal access to opportunities.[43] Some talk about a "right to economic initiative"[44]—and more participation by workers and unions in formulating the policies and institutions that will move societies in that direction. Some think that the level of job creation ought to be made an important measurement of well-being everywhere. Decent work also connects to the concern that in developing countries, the search for more growth to reduce poverty must include a search for the right kind of growth, one that empowers the poor to get the best out of their main asset—their labor (see Chapter 13).[45]

- *New style of work*. People worldwide will increasingly work for many employers at a time through "portfolio working." They will telecommute from great distances (some 30 million in the United States already). They will need to upgrade their knowledge through lifelong learning. And they will have to be able to commute from one pension system to another. A number of new, creative global measures will have to accompany this reinvention of

> the traditional, local labor place into a global labor space. (One such measure, mentioned in Chapter 13, has to do with cross-border accreditation of skills.)

The global thinking has been good at the first level, but progressively less good at formulating the rules for the levels farther down the list. The international resolve behind the four core labor standards has been successful: even countries like Myanmar, which had condoned both forced labor and child labor, have begun to buckle under the pressure of these standards.[46] The standards have also been one of the engines behind the adoption of some 700 voluntary codes of conduct by multinational enterprises.

Yet this success hasn't been followed by equally crisp global thinking about the next three levels. Just as with e-commerce and biotechnology, the underlying phenomenon—in this case the making of a global labor market—is surging way ahead of the world's ability to come up with a minimum set of relevant, helpful, and coherence-creating global rules. To the contrary, clear thinking in the whole area of labor rules took a blow in the recent attempt to link labor standards to the trade rules system—a link that developing countries promptly saw as yet another way for rich countries to keep developing-country products out of their markets.[47]

Migration rules may be in an even worse state of flux. Samuel Huntington, the author of *The Clash of Civilizations,* calls migration the central issue of our time.[48] As we saw in Chapter 2, rich countries face aging and rapidly declining populations, while the developing world will struggle over the next twenty years with intense population pressure and poverty challenges. Developing countries, with more than 95 percent of the world's population increase, will worry about not being able to create enough jobs; rich countries will worry about having too few active workers to sustain growing numbers of elderly dependents. Without immigration, Italy, with one of the world's lowest birth rates, could see its population decline from 58 million to 40 million in the first half of this century. By 2020, Germany will need 1 million immigrants of working age per year simply to maintain its workforce.[49]

More government leaders now understand that the two problems can be solved by enabling, through some sort of global rules, well-paced migration from the poorer to the richer countries. Germany has started a special visa system for information technology workers and is now going beyond this with policies encouraging permanent immigration for the first time. The United Kingdom is also revising its immigration laws. Spain has been looking to Latin America for large-scale population balancing.

But these first moves are a far cry from addressing the emerging global migration pressure. The question is whether the international community will come up with shared migration rules early, or whether it will be panicked into them after a lot of damage is done. This is evident in the following strands:

- *Human smuggling and trafficking.* A burgeoning phenomenon, very much controlled by the underworld, with some 5 million people a year being smuggled and some $10 billion of earnings, this is one of the fastest-growing areas of international criminality. Some global rules are needed because human trafficking feeds not just on poverty but also on the greater restrictions to legal immigration. Because of those tougher restrictions, legal immigration has decreased 25–30 percent in the United States and Europe over the last five years. Rules are also needed because discovery and prosecution risks are kept low due to insufficient international coordination, weak visa and border controls, lax sanctions, and sometimes corruption. This is an urgent global issue—not a week goes by without a disgraceful human tragedy.

- *Asylum rules.* Countries with more open asylum rules end up with a proportionally huge burden—implying the need for a stepped-up global coordination of standards.

- *Migration rules themselves.* The number of countries receiving migrants has increased from forty in 1970 to about seventy today; those supplying migrants, from thirty to fifty-five. Fifteen countries are in both categories. A global labor market is in the making, yet countries have liberalized only trade and investment flows, not migration flows. In fact, immigration laws have become more variegated and restrictive, with little result except for trafficking. The alternative of helping the supplying countries to reduce outbound migration pressure hasn't been followed either—recall the declining aid offered by rich countries since 1990. What's really needed is some sort of global get-together around a positive migration agenda that will be win-win for both the sending and the recipient countries, and that changes the terms of the mostly negative debate about migration so far.[50]

- *Brain drain issues.* Some countries thrive by exporting engineers and scientists—in India it's almost a national business. Yet Jamaica must train more than five doctors just to keep one, and in Botswana, a country where 38 percent of the sexually active population in the fifteen to forty-nine age group is threatened by AIDS, several hundred nurses leave every year for better wages in the United Kingdom.[51] Some sort of global reflection in this area would be welcome, including with respect to taxation. Brain-drain taxes and exit taxes are suspect from a human rights standpoint, but resorting to U.S.-style citizenship-based income taxation could at least help countries recoup some of the education costs incurred for their migrants even after those have left the country.[52]

The labor and migration issues, like the other nineteen issues, bring up one central message: the world has become very small, entangled, and complex, bringing all kinds of global issues to the fore—none of which we can afford to leave unsolved for very long.

PART THREE

Thinking Aloud—New Approaches to Global Problem-Solving

15
No Pilot in the Cockpit

This discussion of twenty inherently global issues is neither final nor comprehensive. For one, I intentionally left defense-oriented security issues out of the list, such as biological weapons, chemical weapons, nuclear arms, and small-arms trade. The security issues, such as conflict and terrorism prevention, that did come up on my list aren't of the same ilk as these more traditional security issues. For the sake of completeness, even those should be part of the full list of global issues.

And others should perhaps be there as well: top pollutants, nuclear safety and proliferation, and perhaps the twin issues of sustainable energy and sustainable agriculture. On the last two, I hesitated quite a bit but came out thinking that their inherently global aspects are already captured by some of the other issues listed—such as global warming and poverty. Hunger is the issue, rather than food, and it is deeply linked to the issue of poverty. The planet won't run out of energy for quite a while, but it's the environmental consequences of its expanded use we must really worry about, with global warming topping the list.

Finally, there are issues like international criminality, crimes against humanity, and more generally the search for a new and broader concept of human rights. These could be the seed for a fourth category, which would be about sharing our *values*.

In any case, I am the first to admit that the list summarized in this book can and should be disputed. Perhaps there are only fifteen or so *truly* global issues, and some of those listed should not be there.

Perhaps, and more likely, there are twenty-five or so, and the final list should indeed contain a fourth category. Incidentally, there has been relatively little conceptual work on how to categorize the various issues—which is a bit alarming, as this intellectual vacuum may itself be an obstacle to the design of new models and methods for global issues management.[1]

But that's not the point. The point is that all the issues I did list share several important characteristics:

- They are planetary, in that some have make-or-break implications for our common future and in that all will create great complications in the relationships among nation-states of this planet if they are not tackled.

- They are urgent global issues. For many of them, every year lost in taking them on brings several years' delay lost in getting them under control—recall the seven-year multiplier of the "dog years" image. And tackling them takes deep, deliberate action—like changing a tanker's course or slowing down a locomotive. Because of this, they must be solved or well on their way to being solved before the next twenty years are over—not in thirty, forty years.

- They are not that expensive to solve in the overall scheme of things. Remember how global warming could be tackled for less than 1 percent of world GDP, how fisheries could be protected and enhanced at the same time, how the effectiveness of aid in fighting poverty could be tripled by changes in approach, how armed conflicts could be more systematically prevented. More important, the cost of remedying global issues is tiny relative to the much bigger long-term cost of not addressing them.

- They are tough. Admittedly, some are harder to solve than others. Some are politically harder to solve. The really tough ones are those whose solution would bring about big global wins but imply big local losses, as well as those that imply high short-term remediation costs when the benefits accrue only over the very long term. In that sense, greenhouse gas emissions (global warming) is clearly tougher to solve than, say, e-commerce rules. At the same time, some issues are technically harder to solve than others. In that respect, rethinking taxation and resolving intellectual property rights problems are actually among the toughest ones. But no issue on the list is easy, either politically or technically—ozone depletion may have been that rare case, and that is why it's not on the list.

- Finally, despite some progress here and there, none of these issues has been decisively and definitively tackled by the current international setup. You'll soon see why.

Also consider this: deep down, these twenty urgent issues are by and large those that are increasingly awakening planetary anxiety—and you can bet that this anxiety will lift to even higher levels as we move further into the next two decades.

For many of these issues, the protesters are ahead of governments in sensing the danger—even though they express themselves mostly in an obstructionist manner and have focused on the trade issue more than on others. And they have a serious point when they say that there's no pilot in the cockpit on such issues. The protesters are also ahead of governments in their activism, even though they are equally short of solution concepts. As Lori Wallach, director of Public Citizens' Global Trade Watch and one of the leaders behind the 1999 WTO protests in Seattle, put it: "How do you have democratic accountability in governance, and enforceable international standards? Either we'll have international rules about that, or we're just going to do it ourselves. That's it."[2]

16
Current Ways of Handling Global Issues Aren't Up to the Job

The complexity of many global issues and their lack of boundaries don't sit well with the territorial and hierarchical institutions that are supposed to solve them: the nation-states.[1] Nation-states know this, and historically their reaction has been to try to respond through treaties and conventions. But they have moved beyond this and created three more contraptions: big intergovernmental conferences, G7-type groupings, and an array of forty or so international institutions that I call "global multilaterals." The international problem-solving setup thus has four parts. Yet none of the parts quite hacks it when it comes to seriously and proactively tackling inherently global issues, and doing it fast.

Treaties and Conventions

Treaties and conventions can work well for bilateral or regional matters but have a very mixed record for global ones. What's more, the ritualistic methods and glacial pace of global treaty making and ratification are not in tune with today's burning global issues, and many of these issues haven't been suitable for treaty making at all.

For the first category of inherently global issues, the environmental or global commons issues, some treaties have generated results. But a large number of them have remained unratified, including the Kyoto Protocol (which still hasn't been ratified at the time of this writing, February 2002, and which won't in any case include the United States). Some are rendered ineffective because of holdouts, such as a UN treaty on marine fish management that did indeed enter into force in December 2001—but with fifteen of the top twenty fishing nations failing to ratify it.[2] Most important, even when ratified, a large number of treaties and conventions suffer from weak commitments or from slow and lax enforcement.[3] In particular, the so-called secretariats set up under many environmental treaties range from nonexistent to weakly funded; few have any enforcement powers. And there are crucial areas where things never got seriously off the ground or ended up half-cocked: the sad story of the Kyoto Protocol is not the only one of its kind. More generally, the contrast between the either insufficient or nonexistent progress on virtually all the issues listed in the first category, and the enormous number of environmental treaties and conventions—some 240, most of them dating from the last forty years—speaks for itself.

Global issues in the second category—those dealing with areas so urgent and so massive as to require global commitments or coalitions for their solution—present the opposite situation, with few treaties and conventions at all. There are some treaties here and there, but mostly glaring holes. And supposed commitments, like the pledge made by the rich countries in the 1970s to give 0.7 percent of their GDPs as official aid, have remained in a studied limbo. Where there have been agreements, they have often been lingering along mostly unratified—as became apparent to everyone the morning after September 11, 2001, in regard to twelve conventions on terrorism.

In the third category—planetary issues requiring global rule making of some sort—about half the issues haven't been addressed through international undertakings at all. Some have been partially addressed by treaties and conventions but with political difficulties that have made progress sometimes incredibly slow: some labor rights conventions

The current international setup for solving inherently global issues (IGIs) is essentially not up to the task . . .

- **Treaties and conventions**
  Too slow for burning IGIs
- **Intergovernmental conferences**
  Too short on follow-up mechanisms
- **G7/8, G-X type groupings**
  Four limitations:
  1. Methodology **3. Knowledge limitations**
  2. Exclusiveness **4. Distance to the people**
- **Global multilateral institutions**
  Not able to handle IGIs alone

FIGURE 16.1 *The Current International Setup*

signed more than twenty years ago still haven't been ratified. By and large, many of the third category of issues are triggered by change itself, and fast change at that: e-commerce, biotechnology, the sudden obsolescence of part of the tax system, the soaring of synthetic drugs, unprecedented and complex challenges around intellectual property rights or the global financial architecture, new migration pressures and needs. Some of these are twenty-first century areas for which the nineteenth-century treaty-making methodology seems out of its depth.

Two more recent developments are likely to further reduce the ability of treaties and conventions to produce prompt solutions to global issues. For one, the new U.S. administration has shown distaste for treaties requiring congressional ratification processes—not just in the case of the Kyoto Protocol but even in other agreements as well. It has, for example, rejected the alternative of amending a thirty-year-old biological weapons convention in favor of direct action not requiring congressional approval.[4]

Second, countries have started to increasingly resort to postponement and language dilution to reach, at almost any cost, some sort of agreement in the eyes of the public at large. The resulting low-grade texts shift the burden onto subsequent, more detailed negotiations. The Doha declaration thus has two instances of "two-phase" processes and addresses the question of agricultural subsidies in a tortured, hedged manner. The agreement reached at the Nice Summit of the EU (see Chapter 17) left so many details for later clarification that on some points, no one is quite sure what was agreed to. The recent fleshing out of the Kyoto Protocol in Marrakesh left uncertainties as to whether penalties for countries breaching emission limits were legally binding or merely a matter of political sanctions.[5]

Given the urgency of today's global issues, these two recent developments do not bode well.[6] At any rate, the limitations and slowness of treaty making are among the reasons the other three parts of the international system have come to the fore, mostly during the second part of the twentieth century: intergovernmental conferences, G7-type groupings, global multilaterals. But on closer inspection, none of them alone seems equipped to handle the twenty global issues, twenty years challenge.

Big Intergovernmental Conferences

Over the last three decades, the UN has mounted heroic rear-guard battles in sustaining the pace of big conferences—each devoted to one particular topic of global importance. All nation-states participate, with each leader generally afforded only five minutes for a statement. These conferences go on for about a week, and some sort of declaration is drafted beforehand and issued at the end. They are often remembered by the city they occurred in: Rio and Kyoto for the environment, Copenhagen and Geneva for social issues, Cairo for population issues, and so on.

But these big, on-and-off conferences have well-known shortcomings. They are too ritualistic, too long on declarations, and too short on follow-up mechanisms—which often boil down to little more than promises to look at the issue again five years down the line. (Kyoto was Rio+5, and in 2002, Rio+10 will happen in Johannesburg). The positioning-and-blame scramble that often precedes these repeat events vividly illustrates the limitations of these conferences. In a nutshell: they are useful for raising awareness about global issues but weak when it comes to effective global problem-solving. And they have lately had a tendency to deteriorate: the September 2001 conference in Durban on racism ended so chaotically that it took another four months to agree on a definitive set of documents.

G7 and Similar Groupings of Countries

Nor do G7 and similar mechanisms provide strong responses to most global issues. Since the mid–1970s, the United States, the United Kingdom, France, Germany, and Japan have been meeting to discuss "major economic and political issues facing their domestic societies and the international community as a whole."[7] A little later, Canada and Italy joined the group, which became the G7. The broad mandate the group has set for itself gives it a lot of defining power, through which it has mobilized its members to take action: consider the calls for debt relief for the poorest countries and against financial havens, and the resolution of the Kosovo crisis, all achievements of the G7 in the last few years.

But its scope is too broad. Recognizing in the 1980s that its mandate was too big and too loose, the G7 began sprouting ministerial forums, task forces, and working groups. In the 1990s, Russia was pulled in, more or less, and the G7 became a sort of G8. Then in 1999, it begat a specialized offspring, the G20—this time to pull in other emerging economies (such as China, India, Mexico, Turkey, Brazil, and others) in response to the global financial crisis.

In a way, that's progress. Yet several limitations remain:

LIMITATION 1: PROCESS. Contrast the way governments worked to create the World Bank and the IMF in 1944 with the way the G7 creates task forces, working groups, communiqués, and other papers, almost always in reaction to problems that have already materialized. The 1944 conference at Bretton Woods, New Hampshire, which led to the birth of those two institutions, pulled together representatives of forty-four rich and poor nations—what a skeptical John Maynard Keynes called "the most monstrous monkey house assembled for years."[8]

Yet the brainstorming at the conference was proactive and genuine. And it took a while—fourteen days in a small town, after sessions in Atlantic City and elsewhere. Great minds were enlisted—Keynes, Harry White, Edward Bernstein, Roy Harrod, Pierre Mendès France. World War II was not over, yet the Bretton Woods visionaries had a sense of urgency about international stabilization, world order, and recovery. So they invented solutions without quite knowing what the problems were.[9] They created a *capacity* to deal with evolving problems.

The G7 and its offspring have other merits, but not that one. So-called "sherpas" negotiate the draft communiqués word by word several months in advance of summits, which are loaded with formal events and photo opportunities that leave little time for proactive brainstorming. In that sense, the G7 has deteriorated over time: its early summit sessions in the 1970s were intimate conversations with genuine personal interactions between leaders, whereas the latest summits have become unwieldy gatherings of thousands of officials. The beleaguered Genoa Summit in July 2001, for example, cost more than $100 million—yet the crucial discussion on the world economy lasted only ninety minutes.

LIMITATION 2: EXCLUSIVENESS. This is hard to remedy. China reportedly declined to join the G7 Okinawa Summit in the summer of 2000, and even in such expanded groupings as the G20, exclusiveness hurts. The G7 said that the G20 was created to "broaden the dialogue on key economic and financial policy issues among systematically significant economies." That's why countries like Brazil, Saudi Arabia, and others are included.[10] But then it excluded the Swiss and the Dutch, who understandably feel left out, particularly as the G20 has been dealing mostly with the issue of crisis prevention and the global financial architecture. The poorest countries, feeling likewise snubbed by such groupings, seek refuge in their own, like the G77. Better a more inclusive gathering like Bretton Woods, no matter Keynes's misgivings.

LIMITATION 3: KNOWLEDGE. Given the complexity of most big global issues, the knowledge base of civil servants dispatched into such groupings by governments could never be strong enough without civil society and business (see Chapter 7). The G7 still has not found a good way to enlist those other sectors: a valiant attempt by Italy, as the G7 chair, to consult civil-society organizations during the preparations for the Genoa Summit met with little success.

LIMITATION 4: DISTANCE. The distance between people at large and the officials in these groupings is very great—the dialogue nil. This was glaringly obvious during the Genoa Summit. Much of the soul-searching since then has been about that.[11]

Global Multilaterals

Nor can global multilateral institutions—those among the international bodies that have global mandates and whose membership includes more or less all countries—tackle inherently global issues alone. These global multilaterals include the United Nations agencies and programs (some forty of them, such as the UN Development Program, the International Labor Organization, the High Commissioner for Refugees, and so many others); the World Bank and the IMF (often jointly referred to as the Bretton Woods institutions); and the World Trade Organization. One could add the Organization for Economic Cooperation and Development which, with some thirty mostly rich member countries, behaves like a global multilateral, even though strictly speaking it isn't one.

Created as part of the postwar world order, the global multilaterals have significant capacities to contribute—largely because they have become unique repositories of specialized knowledge gathered through decades-long worldwide operations. But their roles and their relationships to their owners and overseers—the world's 190-odd nation-states—preclude them from taking on a central role in global problem-solving. They cannot just decide on their own to cut through the tensions and disagreements among their owners.

What's more, most people have a highly exaggerated view of the real power of global multilaterals. They are often very weakly resourced (the WTO's yearly budget is, for instance, below $80 million) and almost always badly overstretched. These days, most of them suffer from low staff morale to boot.

These institutions have also been weakened by constant, debilitating criticism, precisely as concern about global complexity and global issues has mounted: in an age when it is hard to assign blame, they are sitting ducks. Compounding this obfuscation is the way nation-states often passively stand by when global multilaterals get bashed, even though they govern them. Their legitimacy is questioned, in part because their real roles and responsibilities are poorly understood. All this dooms any attempt by any global multilateral to claim a central problem-solving role for itself on any one of the twenty issues.

In sum, none of the four parts of the current international setup looks very promising when it comes to the twenty issues, twenty years challenge. It's not that they aren't doing useful things. It's more that they weren't designed for the kind of urgent global problem-solving needed for the next twenty years of intense change.

Another possible track is a world government. It is worth looking at why it wouldn't work—because the analysis points to an alternative.

17
No Chance for a World Government

The conundrum of the European Union shows why a world government would not be feasible. Despite major achievements, as the EU moves into the complex process of enlarging itself to include many other countries, deep questions have surfaced about its political identity and structure. Following proposals by Jacques Delors, Valéry Giscard d'Estaing, Helmut Schmidt, and others, German Foreign Minister Joschka Fischer launched a major debate in 2000 when he proposed a European federation with a constitution, two parliamentary chambers, an executive, and some sort of "subsidiarity" principle attached to it all, so that EU nation-states would emerge intact. This debate still rages.

As attractive as the federalist idea may be—I am among those who believe it may well be a must for Europe—the vision faces massive challenges:

- The sheer complexity of the arrangements as fifteen, then perhaps twenty-five, then eventually twenty-eight or more EU member states scramble for weight and representation in the new structure.

- The unavoidable distance between people and the new executive that, even with universal suffrage, could widen the already deep gap between EU member-state citizens and Brussels.

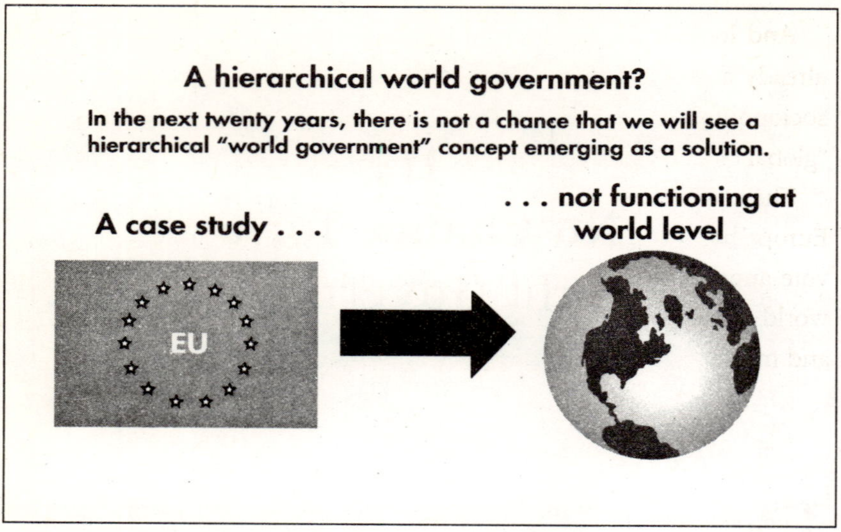

FIGURE 17.1 *A Hierarchical World Government?*

- The likely explosion in "nationality games" in which member countries try to push their own nationals into key leadership positions.

- The gathering of too many issues at the top of the new system—a top likely to be already overwhelmed by the constant need to arbitrate between nation-state bureaucracies and to cater to nation-state egos.

The EU's dilemma shows how hard it would be to achieve a world government in the next twenty years. Today, the EU still has only fifteen members. A world government would have close to 190. Yet, even at the EU level, there are no satisfactory big country–small country arrangements. Look at the unhappy haggling over voting rules at the Nice Summit in December 2000. Now imagine the difficulties at a world level. Using a plausible rule of thumb, we may expect the degree of complication of such arrangements to grow with the square of the number of members. So does the potential for putting off their stakeholders and citizens. De Gaulle called the UN "that thing" *(le machin)*. You can bet that a world government would quickly become "*un grand machin.*"

And look at the question of legitimacy and citizen identity. This is already a problem in the fifteen EU countries, despite shared history, sociopolitical structures, and ambitions. What would it feel like to be a "global citizen" under a world government?[1]

The main point is that there simply isn't enough time to find out. Europe has more time—it deals with its own construction and can devote another few decades to this after the five it has taken so far. The world at large has less time—it must deal with burning global issues, and must do so within the next twenty years.

18
Pointers Towards Solutions: Networked Governance

The foregoing difficulties point to an alternative concept for accelerating the solution of the big global issues. This concept has two generic requirements.

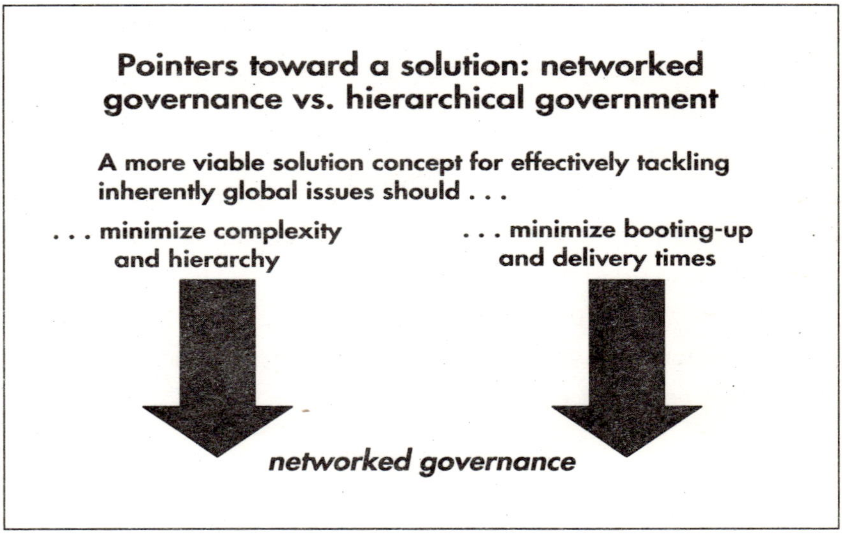

FIGURE 18.1 *Networked Governance Versus Hierarchical Government*

First, complication and hierarchy should be minimized. This requirement has several consequences. For one, each global issue should have its own problem-solving vehicle; this unbundling of the global issues challenge would achieve what scientists call "distributed intelligence." Moreover, membership in the problem-solving vehicle for a given issue should be strongly knowledge related, to minimize excessive layers of incompetence and ritual. Finally, the architecture of the vehicle should be open—it cannot call for a hierarchy that creates distance from the people or is closed to alternatives proposed by "outsiders." People must be able to chime in, and be heard, when they have something to contribute that will deal with the issue at hand.

Second, booting-up and delivery times must be fast. Here again, this has several consequences. Burning global issues cannot wait for the time it takes to negotiate treaties and for the decades it normally takes to ratify them by quorum. Look at where global warming and the world's fisheries will stand in just ten years. So global legislation, which occurs in a very slow public space, cannot be the object of the problem-solving vehicles. These vehicles must operate in another, faster space: that of producing norms and reputational effects (more on this below). And they must capitalize on existing institutions, harnessing the expertise, knowledge, and legislative power of governments and getting the best out of existing multilaterals. There just isn't enough time to set up many new institutions.

These two requirements call for a passage, in global affairs, from traditional hierarchical government to something that looks more like "networked governance."[1]

19
Global Issues Networks

Several solution concepts fit these two prerequisites and the networked governance idea that proceeds from them. One such is to create a new type of public space through global issues networks—each focused on an urgent global issue among the list of twenty. So you'd have twenty or so global issues networks.

What would this look like? Rather than theorize on a concept that is still embryonic, it may be more productive to visualize how such a network could work for a given global issue. At this juncture, imagination is needed more than theory.

Jumping right in, a global issues network could go through three phases:

- a constitutional phase, when the network is convened and set in motion;
- a norm-producing phase, beginning with a rigorous evaluation of options and alternatives; and
- an implementation phase, in which the network takes on a rating role, helping the norms exert their influence through reputational effects.

Each network would be permanent, not on-and-off. Its initially limited membership would increase from phase to phase.[1] And it would keep evolving over its lifetime, which could last for decades.

The Constitutional Phase

The constitutional phase (Figure 9.1) would take a year or so, a duration reminiscent of the Bretton Woods process described above. It would start after a launching event, either an intergovernmental conference—or better, so as not to lose time, a more informal convening event staged by a global multilateral whose specialty and capacity best correspond to the issue at hand. That global multilateral—a UN agency, say—would do this merely as a facilitator, *not* as a problem solver.

Along with the global multilateral, each launch would enlist individuals drawn from three kinds of partners:

- National governments from the developed and developing countries especially concerned by or experienced in the issue and willing to lend some of their most knowledgeable civil servants to the effort for a long period of time. Clout would come not from GDP but from expertise in the issue.

- International civil society organizations—or better, networks of such organizations—able to lend individuals with deep knowledge of the issue and able to represent other civil-society elements in this first stage.

- Firms that have knowledge of the issue and the ability to represent other businesses in this early stage and that can lend highly experienced business leaders to the effort.

More precisely, each network would start with three facilitators: the global multilateral in the lead,[2] one representative selected from the network's civil-society membership, and one representative selected from the business membership. Together they would be in charge of selecting and roping in the first members (a tricky task), convening the

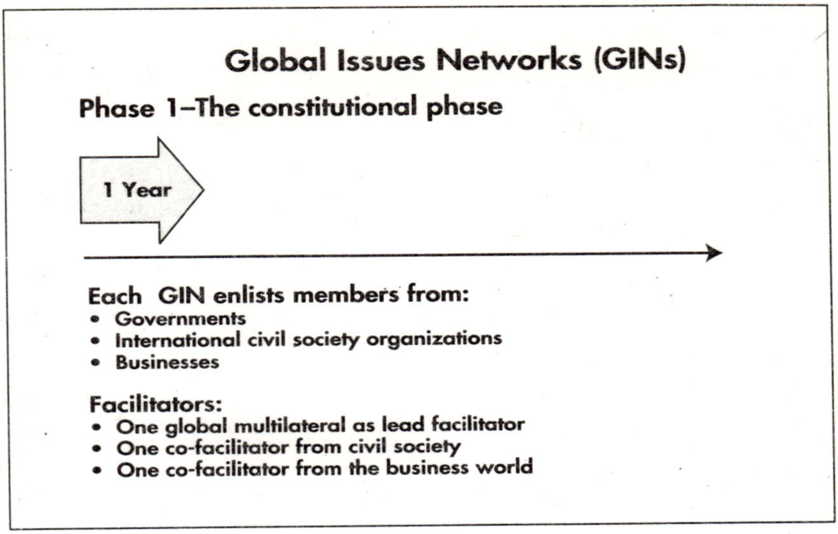

FIGURE 19.1 *Global Issues Networks—Phase 1*

early events, raising financing, and organizing the knowledge base. As facilitators, they would in effect be at the heart of what in the Internet world is called an "open-source project," setting up and moderating open-horizon, permanent efforts spanning as many years as needed.

During the constitutional phase, a key task for each network would be to adopt its own code of conduct (some elements are illustrated below). The network would also link up with other global issues networks and share in best practices on how to organize, how to operate, how to communicate.

The Norm-Producing Phase

As the network enters this next phase (Figure 19.2), it would increase its membership and engage in the production of norms, standards, or policy recommendations. Depending on the issue, this phase could last two to three years, maybe longer. First, a few words on the *methodology* to be used.

The main challenge for global issues networks will be to represent various dimensions of knowledge and points of view—but only among members whose problem-solving contribution will be real and substantial. There must be discipline in this. Parties that come merely to state their position but aren't willing or able to engage in the open-minded brainstorming and exploration of options required for global problem-solving would dial themselves out, even if they made it into the network at first. Similarly, a member may have come in as a business, government, or civil-society representative, but once in, must think and act as a global citizen, not as a staunch defender of a narrow interest. This discipline must be spelled out in the network's own code of conduct and enforced by the facilitators.

Picture this discipline not so much as sheer toughness but as the outcome of an environment in which the network will get the best out of its members. To that effect, the network must make a constant appeal to universal values, not just in the broad sense in which the philosopher Kant meant it but in terms of the more specific values that are a prerequisite to the solution of the global issue at hand. Members must be required to state their opinions publicly and to always link them to the problem-solving process. Is it a pure dream to imagine people behaving as global citizens in such an environment? No: research actually shows that in the right environment, people can be extraordinarily fair (for example, when it comes to allocating something scarce) and can quickly come to see selfishness as extremely embarrassing.[3]

The second point of methodology: networks would strive for "rough consensus"—a concept taking shape in the Internet world. It means that there is enough agreement on fundamentals to get down to policy work or norm production—whatever the problem requires. It's a work-in-progress concept, not a voting one.[4]

Finally, to help get to that point, each network would create a potentially vast electronic town meeting as an adjunct—with an entirely open architecture aimed at enlisting all interested parties in the network's work through "deliberative polling." The Internet's huge mobilizing potential would be harnessed for this, but the process must remain disciplined—each set of alternatives subject to polling would have to move the diagnostic or problem-solving process ahead, even if only by an inch. This discipline would also be in the network's code of conduct.

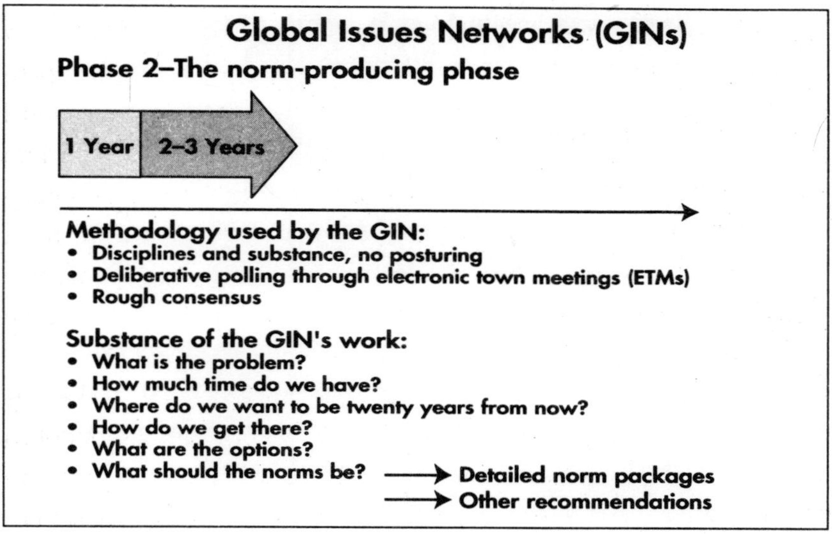

FIGURE 19.2 *Global Issues Networks—Phase 2*

Some networks may also decide to set up an independent expert panel as another adjunct—borrowing from a technique that has often worked in the treaty-making world (recall the IPCC in Chapter 12). It is important that experts be outside the network itself, to preserve scientific independence.[5]

So much for methodology. As for the *substance* of its work, each network, with the help of its electronic town meeting and independent expert panel adjuncts, would go through a sequence of tasks:

- It would start by scoping the issue, defining its major elements and sub-elements, mapping the causalities, and describing the planetary downside.

- It would figure out how much time is left for denting the issue (each has its own time dynamic).

- Its members would put themselves in the place of their children twenty years from now, describing how the issue had been tackled.

The electronic town meeting would be crucial for this, with the polling focused in this case on alternatives for describing each item.

- The network would extrapolate a vision of the situation twenty years down the line and then work back to the intermediate steps needed to realize that vision, figuring out who would have to take these steps.

- Next—and this is the toughest job—the network would draw up a set of norms or standards to set in motion the processes that will lead to the fulfillment of these intermediate steps. While these norms and standards will generally be the main output of the network, it may also need to make recommendations for complementary mechanisms, like funding or compensation facilities, monitoring systems, and intergovernmental regulatory setups.[6]

- Norms and standards will, however, almost always be at the heart of a network's output, and at the heart of the concept of global issues networks. They could be packed together, or they could apply in specified ways to various players, such as nation-states, businesses, even multilaterals. For one, the network would specify the norms according to which nation-states should pass national legislation in regard to the issue in question. It could even enjoin countries to ratify existing treaties, if some useful ones are on hand, and ask them to make sure that these treaties will be enforced. It would specify norms for businesses to follow as they operate across the globe. It could come up with some sort of norms for global multilaterals operating in that field—asking them to set up whatever funding or other mechanism may be needed on top of the other things, or even sometimes telling them how to get their act together with respect to the issue at hand. And so forth—picture this set of norms as a highly specific, functional ethos for the entire global issue area in question.[7]

- Finally, this norm package (or packages, as noted earlier) would then be put forward through a launch event. Some people like to

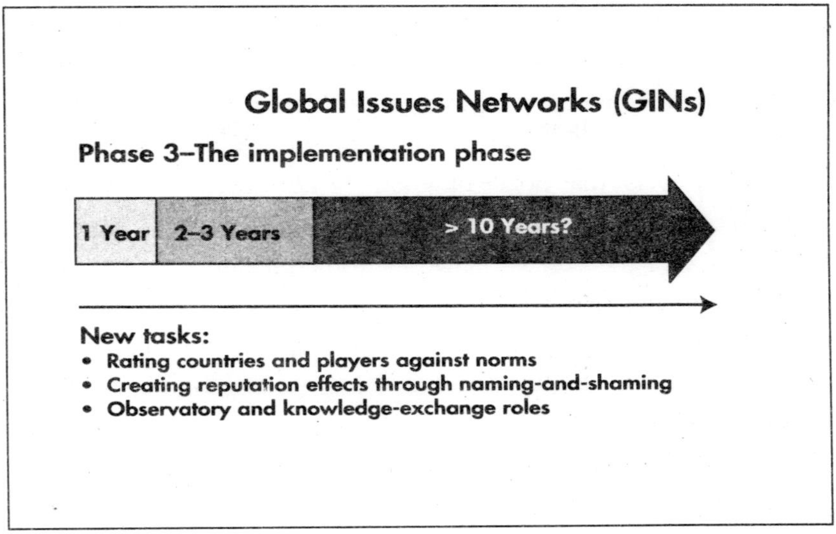

FIGURE 19.3 *Global Issues Networks—Phase 3*

refer to norms as "soft law," but as the implementation phase will show, their use would be anything but soft.

The Implementation Phase

In this third phase (Figure 19.3), which could last ten years or more, each network would further increase its membership and turn into a rating vehicle—evaluating countries and other relevant players (such as businesses) on how well they follow the norms or standards, perhaps even along the lines of the ISO 9000 practices pioneered by the International Organization for Standardization.[8] They would also regularly rate players for the strongest improvements from one year to the next. Reputational effects would now come into play: the network and electronic town meeting would now spend their time tracking how stakeholders do or do not follow suit. The more the global issues network looks like an activist NGO in that phase, the better.

But remember: norms are not legislation. For the most part, their realization would hinge on countries freely deciding—on their own or under the pressure of reputational effects—to enact conforming legislation.

Nor would networks have regulatory authority over business or other civil society players. What they would have is moral authority, and they would have to come up with ways of wielding it—through exposure, disclosure, and reputation effects—in short, through naming-and-shaming "rogue players" that violate or ignore the norms. This isn't hard to do in our media age: the press loves league tables as much as those rated fear them—and global issues networks would provide a lot of copy.

Is there any evidence that reputational effects will have any influence? As we saw in chapter 14, exposing countries in money laundering lists has had an almost immediate salutary effect. Another example, altogether different but very telling: in Indonesia, the government authorities had few enforcement means with respect to environmental violations by businesses. They created a five-tier ranking for companies: from gold for those that go beyond compliance to black for egregious violators. The top rankers get public applause, and the worst offenders get six months to improve before their names are made public. Guess what: most of the latter have scrambled to invest in remedial technologies for fear of public exposure. Expect global issues networks to operate much in the same way on the global scene.

If simple issue-by-issue exposure and reputation effects proved insufficient, there would be many other possibilities. Global issues networks could gang up and produce multi-issue ratings for all countries—to sharpen the distinction between countries that are good norm-following citizens of the planet, and those free-riding ones that aren't following up on norms through national legislation or treaty ratification. In this way, the "rogue state" concept would end up expanded in an intriguing way. One could even imagine the UN having something to do with establishing and even sanctioning these overall scores. Even without that, the broader definition of rogueness could have considerable mileage.

Finally, besides engaging in rating activities and promoting reputational effects, the networks would also become a best practice exchange system, with their electronic town meeting adjuncts functioning as observatories and knowledge exchanges. Here's a final snapshot of global issues networks with their increasing membership from phase to phase:

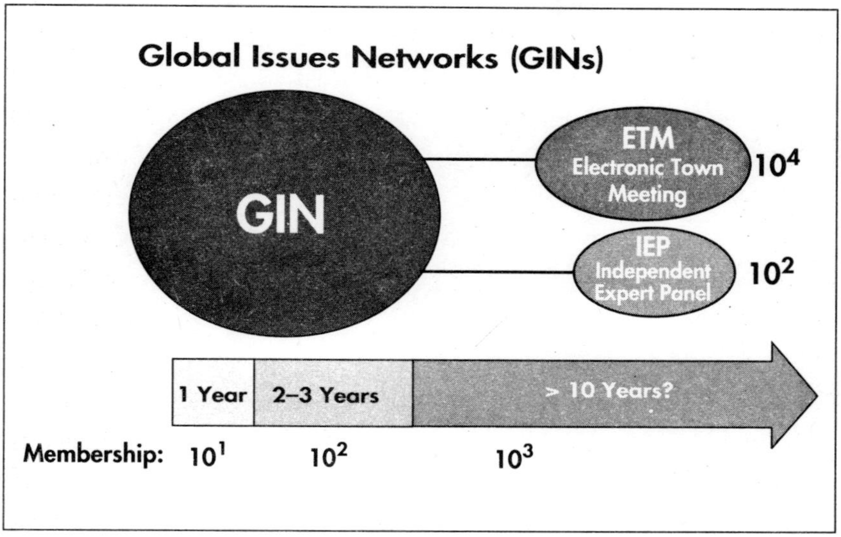

FIGURE 19.4 *Global Issues Networks—Recap*

Membership starts in the tens, moves to the hundreds in the second phase, and finally to the thousands. The electronic town meeting can enlist tens of thousand participants or more—there is no real limit. Where an independent expert panel exists as well, it could enlist several hundred experts, or more—the IPCC has 1,057.

20
Good Things About Global Issues Networks

Global issues networks are a messy concept.[1] But this messiness heralds great flexibility in adapting basic methods to the specifics of each issue and over time. I could go on and on, imagining new details and variations. But the visualization here—that's all it claims to be—is enough to show the general idea and its strengths and weaknesses.

Global issues networks embody four overriding themes that, in one way or another, could advance the state of global problem-solving.

Speed

The networks are geared to rapid norm production and rapid activation of reputational effects. That's why there is a practical "let's-get-down-to-work" immediacy to the methods described here. What are the issues? How much time do we have? What would be the vision of a successful effort twenty years out? How would we get there? What are the options? How do the options come out in polling? Contrast this with the time lost in moral pontificating, overly abstract statements, and vacuous calls for action that characterize much of the record on global issues so far.

Another speed effect: through the political energy and urgency that they will generate, networks will pressure the existing international system into responding at a much faster pace than it would naturally adopt.

Legitimacy

As German philosopher Jürgen Habermas observed, global governance means designing domestic policies for and at the level of the planet.[2] But he points out that there is a serious obstacle to doing this. In national politics, domestic policy discussions take place in the ambience of a shared political ethos and culture, making for relatively "dense" communications.[3] To communicate as effectively on the international stage, citizens would need to develop a sort of global identity—not an easy thing to do.

Global issues networks, together with their electronic town meetings, begin to overcome this obstacle. How?

- First, building a network around a single global issue maximizes the chances of mobilizing people around a shared concern, if not an ethos. Global citizenship has a better chance of developing issue by issue than across the board.

- Second, the networks, with their open architecture, would engage people from all over the world and from all relevant constituencies in such activities as formulating norms and participating in rating rounds. This would promote the sort of global citizenship-building and formation of a common ethos that Habermas and others argue is essential to global problem-solving.

- Third, the electronic town meetings would also add something brand new. In a world where Internet communications have killed the old trade-off between the reach and the richness of messages (see Chapter 4), the virtual public space they create could go a long way towards reducing the distance between people and policymakers. This would address one of the fault points in the current international setup.

What might emerge is a new basis of legitimacy. Habermas suggests that it would be less exigent than the legitimacy traditionally attached to democratic representation. I wonder if it might not in a sense be more exigent, as it would have to wed criteria of participation, scientific understanding, and the common good in ways never seen before.

The legitimacy that global issues networks bring is a *horizontal legitimacy* emerging from joint deliberations—across borders and across government, business, and civil society—by a large group of people deeply concerned and knowledgeable about one issue. It would not at all replace but rather complement the other legitimacy—the *vertical legitimacy* of the traditional local-to-global electoral processes of nation-states, which deals with all issues, but within the confines of a defined territory.

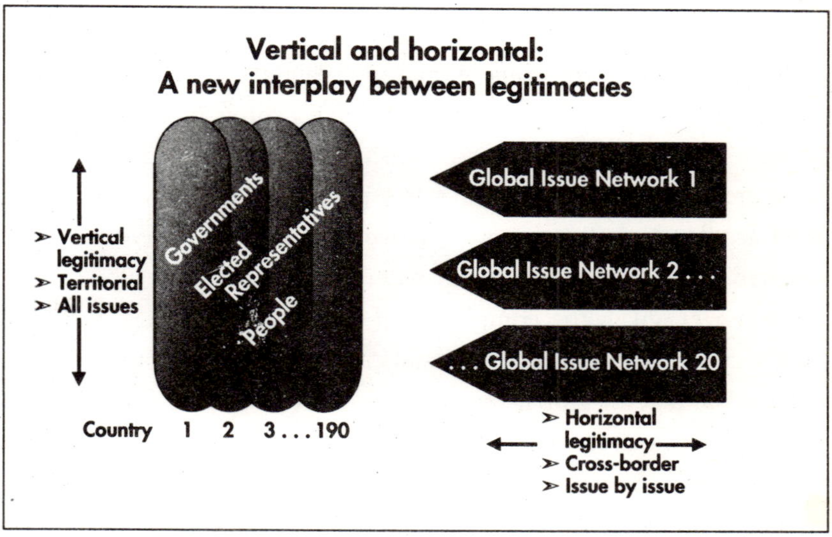

FIGURE 20.1 *Vertical and Horizontal: A New Interplay Between Legitimacies*

Here's a way to see how the two dovetail: the horizontal legitimacy of the global issues networks is designed precisely to pressure the traditional vertical legitimacy systems of nation-states into performing better on urgent planetary issues. Performing better means acting faster, and with more of a long-term, global citizenship perspective than those traditional systems normally come up with.

At the same time, expect the horizontal legitimacy system to impose on the political systems of nation-states an accountability framework that is currently lacking. Short-term-oriented, territorially minded traditional politicians would now have to reckon with something bigger, something more issues-focused than the kudos or disapproval of their local constituency. The result, potentially, is a new way of judging politicians.

Diversity

By design, networks would involve three parties that often have different vantage points: public, private, and international civil-society organizations. The power of the knowledge contributions from such variegated players is a definite advantage over the current international setup. Experiments by some global multilaterals with such tri-sector partnerships (in areas not strictly global) show how fruitful this process can be. A tri-sector partnership I helped set up a few years back around the issue of traffic safety in the developing world (where road accidents can cost up to 2 percent of GDP) quickly took more creative tracks than if each sector had tried to experiment alone.

Moreover, given the complexity of today's global issues, both private-sector players and international civil-society organizations have a clear advantage of global reach—and often of greater knowledge—over civil servants from national governments. I have also been repeatedly struck by how much easier it is to engage global business leaders in long-term global thinking than government leaders bound by short electoral cycles or overwhelmed by the excessive number of issues they are supposed to be wise about (see Chapter 7 on both points).

Civil-society organizations possess similar knowledge advantages, particularly when they form international networks between themselves. One could expect the existence of global issues networks to prompt civil-society players to form multiple networks just for the purpose of participation. Recent experience (such as that with debt relief or trade) shows how such networks can quickly acquire expertise surpassing that of traditional experts.

An interesting by-product could come with this. As we saw in Chapter 7, many question the raw legitimacy of civil society, calling it unrepresentative, only to end up incapable of spelling out the consequences of having said this. But global issues networks, with their peculiar methodology and membership system, offer a way for at least some elements of civil society to migrate beyond that raw legitimacy into a more sanctioned, acknowledged form of legitimacy—for those of its representatives who manage, through the knowledge and perspective they bring, to make it into a network and to stay engaged in its problem-solving activities. The same applies to business, whose legitimacy in global problem-solving could otherwise be questioned in the same way.

Compatibility with Traditional Institutions

Global issues networks and their electronic town meetings are both soft and hard. As we saw, they are hard in that they will use the sledgehammer of ratings and reputational effects—much more potent devices than even rules or sanctions.

But they are soft in that they are open, flexible creatures that tolerate and even need traditional institutions. Global issues networks need the current international setup (described in Chapter 16), despite its shortcomings. Why? Because governance needs government.[4] As we saw, networks may well need a traditional intergovernmental conference as a launching event. And since they won't legislate, they will need nation-states' legislatures to pass laws in line with the norms they set. Also, if they ended up recommending funding or other facilities, the help of global multilaterals may well be a must.

In effect, global issues networks are in the business of getting the best out of the existing international setup. This is a far better alternative than trying to create new institutions or to engage in endless reforms of those that exist—which would take exactly what the world doesn't have: a lot of time.

Networked Governance

Global issues networks thus come out of a concept that may well be of this age: networked governance. This will not be a bed of roses. Expect messiness, ambiguity, and corner-cutting. But also expect speed, action, and a novel source of horizontal legitimacy independent of, but highly complementary to the vertical legitimacy that underpins traditional representation processes.

As suggested in Part One, the new world economy could easily be described, and indeed has been described by some, as a "networked economy." There is a compelling logical symmetry (even a touch of poetic justice) in juxtaposing "networked governance" to it. This juxtaposition is one of the ways through which we can raise the human institutions line (in the parlance of Figure 8.1 in Chapter 8) in response to the crisis of complexity created by the two big forces that will so profoundly change the world in the twenty years to come.

That concept of networked governance, described here through *one* variety—global issues networks with their electronic town meetings and expert panel adjuncts—is not taken out of thin air: it strongly relates to the three new realities discussed in Chapter 7.

21
Controversial Aspects

As always, the devil will be in the details. Worse, it could even be in the overall design itself. At least four major pitfalls await networked governance and the global issues network idea that illustrates what it could look like.

The Sheer Complexity of the Tasks

Almost by definition, all twenty global issues present formidable challenges in producing global norms. As discussed earlier, they are all either politically difficult or technically difficult, or more likely both. While there may be the occasional win-win solution for many aspects of global issues, much of the problem-solving involves global wins and local losses, or immediate sacrifices for the benefit of people not yet born. Think of global warming and the carbon emission ceilings.

But the degree of difficulty is inherent in the issues to be solved, not in the network approach. If an issue is tough, it will be tough for the current international setup to handle, and it will likewise make life hard for any global issues network that would try its hand at it. Yet if anything, the networks and their practical approach (where simply asserting individual positions isn't accepted and where the members must think like global citizens) may have a better chance of delivering solutions than the current international setup left to its own devices. Put it another way: what's the alternative?

Legitimacy and Democratic Representation

Who decides who will join a global issues network? Which civil society outfits or networks will be deemed to represent others and who says they do? Which business firms? Who will be expelled for failure to adopt a global citizen approach in problem-solving? By whom? These sorts of questions, the hardest by far, rightfully pile up around the network concept—particularly during the tricky constitutional phase. Moreover, people will remark, the networks are born and live outside the electoral system.

Once more: what's the alternative? The current international setup isn't delivering solutions on time. And global government is not feasible in the twenty years or so we have to bring the major global issues under control.

But other responses to the legitimacy question can also vindicate the concept:

- Global networks are not legislative bodies. They would set forth norms and rate players against them. Since they are not a form of government, but a kind of governance tool, the democratic representation argument loses in cogency.

- The three facilitators of each network will have to ensure that other questions about representation are acceptably answered. Among those, the global multilaterals acting as lead facilitators for the various networks will have a special role to play. And they are, in a way, reasonably well equipped to do that. Their technocratic quality, often seen by outsiders as a liability, would here be an asset precisely because they have less of an axe to grind than representatives from governments, businesses, or civil society. Together with the other two facilitators, they would be well placed to help the network agree on a balanced membership and marshal the knowledge contributions of the various players. And their global membership would enable them to do a good job at bringing in representatives from the poorest countries and constituencies, which might otherwise lack voice and links to global networks.

- As we saw in Chapter 19, networks would be built on firm principles for inclusion or exclusion of members. What is the player's contribution of knowledge on the issue? Is the player acting and thinking as a global citizen or merely representing himself? The three facilitators will have much power, and much responsibility, in adjudicating this under the code of conduct adopted by the networks.

- The electronic town meetings—wide-open on-line polling platforms—may bring a greater element of democratic participation than the traditional local-to-global pyramid of electoral processes. You could well have huge numbers of qualified people from across the world chiming in on issues they know something about. In that sense, these adjuncts to the networks are enormously important: they help global issues networks build a novel form of horizontal, global-citizenship-related legitimacy that complements the traditional vertical legitimacy systems existing within nation-states.

- Finally, imagine a setup in which the UN would ask all its members to stage a referendum once a network's norm packages have reached some sort of threshold in national legislation—say, when they have been enacted in half the member states. This is an idea proposed in discussions of what a "world government" could look like,[1] but networked governance offers many more avenues for creativity. If this sort of idea were to work, the networks would become just the first stage, the chrysalis, of a more traditional global legislative process—one meant to spread its wings in a global manner with and through the UN. That could be a good outcome: the network's work-in-process legitimacy would perhaps be temporarily questionable to some or many, but its final legitimacy would be bestowed by the formal adoption of its ideas.[2]

Linkages Between Issues

Setting up one global network for each global issue promises faster, more focused problem-solving but has one major drawback: linkages between issues could get lost. For example, there are complex two-way interactions between poverty and environmental issues. Global warming and fisheries depletion will hurt poor people the most; in turn, poverty worsens such global issues as biodiversity loss, deforestation, and infectious diseases. Environmental issues also interact directly among themselves: global warming may aggravate water deficits and biodiversity losses. And poverty and education issues are strongly interlinked. We even saw a link between reinventing taxation and the environment, through carbon taxes. Conflict prevention will be harder if something isn't done about water deficits. And on and on. So linkages do matter.

Yet it would be silly to abandon the issue-by-issue approach of global issues networks because of the linkage problem—for two reasons. The first reason can be found in a profound book, *Notes on the Synthesis of Form,* by architect Christopher Alexander. He shows how problem-solving, to be effective, must go through the identification of subsystems or issues that are reasonably independent of each other. By contrast, bundling subsystems or issues together to an excessive extent is a sure way to miss out on the solution.[3]

The second reason for hanging on to the issue-by-issue approach is that it spares the world one of the nastier practices of world diplomacy—the tendency for negotiators to trade laxity on one issue against laxity on another, or to contrive the merger of two issues so as to better paralyze the solution of one of them. Specialists in conflict resolution believe that such linkage tactics can facilitate negotiations, but when it comes to global problem-solving around burning planetary issues, the more likely result from such tactics is just what the planet does not need—half-a-loaf solutions based on low-grade problem-solving.

But then, what to do about the linkage problem? At a discussion of this dilemma at the Santa Fe Institute, physicist Murray Gell-Mann and some of his colleagues suggested a kind of twenty-first global issues network that would serve as the connector between issues and the networks working on them. In the same way that global issues networks would exchange best practices among themselves and even gang up to produce multi-issue ratings of countries, they are likely to interact on linkages. But this will indeed happen far more systematically and conscientiously if the process is facilitated by a twenty-first network, different as it would be from the other twenty.

The Simplistic Appearance of It All

If you read some of the technical literature on global governance—dense, abstract, self-referential—my description of how global issues networks might look and feel like is bound to appear naive. Just like the concept of networked governance. It's hard to answer that criticism—except by asking whether the *real* naïveté doesn't lie in believing that the current international setup has any chance of delivering global solutions in time.

Beyond that, there are some precedents that show that the idea may not be so simplistic after all. These precedents are far from the global issues networks discussed here, but they possess the virtue of having experimented with the tri-sector approach. One is the Global Dams Commission, which in the last few years has managed, despite some lingering controversy and stumbling along the way, to come up with norms that can help decide whether a particular large dam is a good or bad dam. This may not be an inherently global issue, and the commission's methodology wasn't that of a global issues network as described here, but it shows that tri-sector work can yield prompt results: some governments immediately started to reexamine their support to certain dams. Another still ongoing example has to do with sustainable forestry and equally involves the three sectors.

Debate is still going on about these partial precedents—which already suggest some do's and don'ts. There is also, in a way, the precedent of the International Labor Organization, one of the oldest global multilaterals. It has resorted to a tri-sector approach for decades (in this case, government, employers, unions), even though its methodology remains more traditional and ritualistic than that envisioned for global issues networks.

On the norms-producing aspect of global issues networks, there are also some precedents. As we saw, the savvy approach of the Financial Action Task Force has made many countries want to escape from its list of money-laundering nations established on the basis of forty criteria, to the point where half of the listed countries enacted the necessary legislation within a year or so. There is a similar process for evaluating offshore centers on the safety of their financial system, through the so-called Financial Stability Forum. The OECD publishes a list of egregious tax havens. And a specialized NGO, Transparency International, produces annual ratings of countries in terms of corruption.

There are many other examples. But none of these norms have gained the legitimacy that global issues networks would confer through their tri-sector participation and peculiar methodology. Actually, in the absence of this legitimacy, some countries have badly resented the imposition of criteria by rich countries on others—as in the case of money laundering and egregious tax havens. Global issues networks and their methodology thus build on recent, embryonic naming-and-shaming experiments, while marking an improvement on them.

22
Stepping Back: Other Solutions Besides Global Issues Networks

Global issues networks are not the only shape networked governance could take. Nor are they the only solution to accelerating global problem-solving. While I have spent a bit of time selling the idea of global issues networks concept, there are two more categories of ideas worth thinking about, not of the network governance family but with some links to it.

The G20 Track

One idea would be to keep the issue-by-issue approach but to stop short of setting up tri-sector global issues networks with their peculiar methodology—by sticking to the more traditional (I would even say pedestrian) approach of G-something groupings of countries. Here's the idea: you could set up for each of the twenty or so global issues a corresponding G20. Just as the one G20 in existence deals mostly with the issue of the world's financial architecture and is populated by finance ministers,[1] you could have one G20 per global issue, each gathering the relevant technical ministers.

The existing G20 includes the G7 countries, the country that happens to hold the six-month EU presidency, plus Australia, China, India, Indonesia, Korea, Russia, Turkey, Saudi Arabia, Mexico, Brazil, Argentina, and South Africa. If you had one G20 per global issue, each would have a different country composition, but always with the same G7 core.

Even though the existing G20 has remained mostly a dialogue forum (with many decisions being taken by the G7 and a related technical group called the G10), nothing would prevent other G20s from producing something close to the global norms and other recommendations that the global issues networks would produce. Of course, G20s would be more on-and-off than the permanent global issues networks. They would not come with the strange, novel form of legitimacy that networks bring with their tri-sector, cross-border communities. Nor would they find it easy to exploit the novel methodology described for the networks. And clearly, G20s would share in the four limitations of G7-type groupings at large described in Chapter 16. But less palatable as they are, they have the merit of practical simplicity.

The New Diplomacy Track—and Expanded Concept of Aid

Some thinkers in and around the UN Development Program (UNDP), notably Inge Kaul, have suggested ideas that could usefully complement the global issues network or G20 tracks. In a nutshell, they involve an expanded concept of diplomacy and aid.[2] Here are some of the things they would involve:

- Creating, within the technical ministries of all nation-states—say, agriculture, energy, education, and so on—expert-diplomats who deal directly with their foreign counterparts on global issues.

- Equipping such ministries with two budgets rather than just one: one for domestic programs (C budget, for "country") and one for global action (G budget, for "global").

- Similarly, dividing official development aid into C and G budgets.

- Setting up a global participation fund to help developing countries, particularly the poorest, participate more genuinely in global problem-solving.

What Could Well Happen

Imagine some sort of private brainstorming among the leaders of the world, not on the global issues themselves—they would quickly drown in the complexity of it all—but on the question of the global problem-solving methodology. There could be many outcomes to such a debate, but you could bet that one of the possible outcomes would look roughly like this:

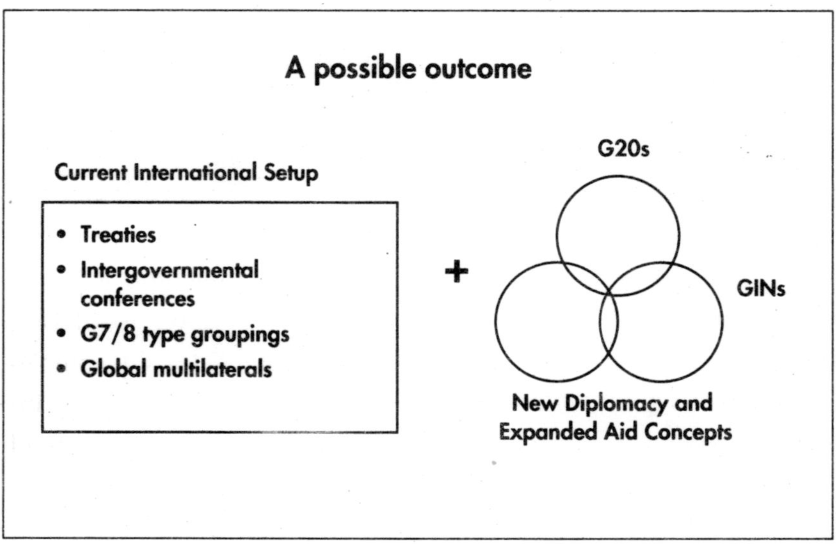

FIGURE 22.1 *A Possible Outcome*

That is to say, a potentially viable structure could be one where the current international setup is not replaced, but instead intentionally energized, put under pressure, and made more accountable through a mixture of three new things: global issues networks (labeled GINs in the figure above) for some issues; G20s for others; and the interesting, farseeing UNDP ideas on new diplomacy and expanded aid being applied more generally. This would not be a bad outcome, even if it isn't very neat, and even if the G20 ingredient harks back, perhaps unhelpfully, to some of the old way of thinking.

In some ways, the threesome above would even have some real synergies. For one, both global issues networks and G20s would have a better chance of functioning if in parallel, the UNDP ideas developed a favorable terrain for them to be successful. In particular, as the solution to all of the twenty global issues described above will require local implementation, much of it in developing countries (remember from Part Two how solving some of the twenty issues called among other things for higher aid levels), the G aid budget and the global participation fund ideas would become very relevant—perhaps even a must.

Other Proposals, Including Some That Are Unlikely to Work

Ideas have been floated lately on setting up a world parliament;[3] creating an Economic Security Council at the UN;[4] increasing the G7 to a G16 or even to a global G20;[5] expanding the G7 to include representatives from major regional trading areas;[6] or launching a Global Governance Group of twenty-four members.[7] There are many variations around these themes. Among those ideas, expanding the G7 sounds like a reasonable improvement on the "current international setup" of Figure 22.1 above—and so would perhaps some sort of Economic Security Council. But many of these ideas are headed towards the immediate, lethal overload that comes from trying to accommodate *all global issues* under one problem-solving or debating vehicle. Just picture the sessions of a world parliament.

Also, consider the following, perhaps unusual way of looking at this: our world may well be emerging from a period of East-West tension into a period of North-South tension, combined with a tension between people who thrive on change and people who fear or hate change. If this prediction is right, then there are far more opportunities to address those tensions through issue-by-issue approaches (global issues networks or even the threesome above) than through global, all issues–encompassing contraptions like world parliaments or large-mandate but small-membership bodies. In fact, some of those are far more likely to aggravate these tensions than to calm them down.

23
Conclusion: Imagination and a Different Type of Thinking

Never have there been such massive opportunities for improving the human condition. Yet never has there been such uncertainty about our ability to grasp these opportunities. Protesters sense the rising anxiety and are speaking out. People everywhere are looking for some dramatic change in the way global problems get addressed—particularly since the U.S. decision to take distance from the Kyoto Protocol and after the events of September 11, 2001, both of which were real eye-openers. Deep down, people sense that there's a wonderful upside, but also a terrific downside to the way the planet is evolving. Intuitively, they sense that time is running out—that it is high noon.

It is precisely in times like these that the messy concepts of networked governance and of global issues networks could become viable: the networks' speed and flexibility fit well with the many issues at hand and the short time to solve them. And as we saw, for some issues, it may be simpler to start a G20-type group. You could say that these are all improvised, less-than-perfect solutions. But as Karl Polanyi, one of the most insightful observers of big social changes, mused more than half a century ago: "Not for the first time in history may makeshifts contain the germs of great and permanent institutions."[1]

At any rate, what's needed is imagination, and a different type of thinking. New thinking about how government, business, and civil society ought to work together and about how to coax nation-states into passing legislation in the interest of the planet, not just their own local constituencies. New thinking about network-like setups that create, global issue by global issue, a sort of horizontal, cross-border source of legitimacy that complements the traditional vertical representation processes and legitimacy of nation-states. New, Internet-inspired thinking about getting many people to chime in via the new technologies and to embrace something that begins to look like global citizenship. In short, we need out-of-the box thinking.

But we also need some really fast thinking. For many urgent global issues, the turnaround time is now, in the next two decades, not over the next half century—think, for instance, of global warming, fisheries, infectious diseases, synthetic drugs, and biotechnology rules.

Those were more or less the messages of Part Three.

Part Two was designed to give you a quick overview of the twenty major global issues—not in a definitive way but as a bridge between Part Three and Part One.

Part One had the most important, context-setting messages. The main one was that besides fast thinking, some straight thinking also would not hurt. It is amazing to see how easily people trap themselves into confused thinking through words like "globalization" or "antiglobalization." These broad, mushy terms are a sure path to wrong guesses, wrong diagnoses, and wrong solutions.

I have tried to suggest that the way out is to step back and look at the two separate forces that will deeply change the world in the next two decades—the population increase that will stretch the planet to its limits, and the new world economy that means doing virtually everything differently. These forces bring a long list of stresses besides some wonderful opportunities. And these stresses promise a sort of crisis of complexity—as societal issues become more complex, the rate of change truly breathtaking, and human institutions more and more handicapped by the snail-like pace at which they evolve.

The big issue of our time is right there: raising the game of these human institutions and particularly of those in charge of public governance—groupings of governments, nation-state governments, government units, global multilaterals, other international institutions. Without this, the crisis of complexity's nasty twin, the crisis of governance, will sour things up for sure. The kind of bad mood already visible in so many areas of public debate is a harbinger of this.

But raising the game of human institutions cannot happen merely through reform of a few existing institutions. One of the tragedies of our times is the widespread belief that we need only reform a couple of existing international organizations, and presto! all will be fine. Many politicians and protesters have fallen into that trap.

The job is bigger than this: it has to do with addressing, beyond the few and marginal successes the world has witnessed, the basic, undeniable failure of the *entire* international setup and the world's nation-states at the task of fast and effective global problem-solving. And the solution requires thinking in terms of the three new realities that accompany the crisis of complexity—the moves away from hierarchies, away from the obsolete territorial instincts of nation-states, and away from the artificial separation between government, business, and civil society.

This is where the three parts of this book connect, and it is here that the concepts of networked governance and global issues networks find their source. Think about them, and they may grow on you—even if, like me, you feel some discomfort about this or that feature of this approach.

Remember, too, that thinking differently brings its pitfalls. I myself have undoubtedly fallen into a few, but in the search for better, faster global problem-solving approaches, this is a necessary price to pay. But I'd rather have tripped you up by this or that flaw in my thinking than have misled you into believing that the current international setup, or any minor reform of it, will deliver the goods alone. It won't.

Postscript

Upon completing this short book, I have two regrets and one request.

My first and real regret is that due to the book's topic and structure, I was not able to give China and India the space they deserve. Half the population of the developing world lives in those two giant countries, and how they respond to the twenty global issues over the next twenty years will matter enormously. It's almost worth another book.

My second, more mitigated regret is that I may have unfairly spent more time hinting at what has not been happening in global problem-solving than paying homage to what has been attempted. As an international civil servant myself, I know only too well what kind of back-breaking and thankless workloads global affairs can bring. I would therefore have quite a bit of empathy for those leaders, ministers, diplomats, and international civil servants who may feel that I have described the glass as half empty when I ought to have described it as half full. Yet I'll stop short of apologizing, as I won't abandon my basic position, which is that when it comes to fast and effective global problem-solving, the glass is less than half full.

Finally, here comes my request. I thrive on two things: examples of what's going on from ripped-out newspaper clippings and live questions or suggestions from audiences. Looking back, they have helped me change or improve on my thinking on global problem-solving far more than any of the scholarly articles or books I may have read on the topic. So if you want to send questions, ideas, or examples my way, I'd be delighted to receive them on a site set up for this purpose at http://www.rischard.net. Even if I cannot respond to all of them, I'll do my best to post or react to those that have jostled my line of thinking or added a new idea or perspective.

July 2001 to February 2002

Endnotes

Part One

Chapter 2

1. See successive United Nations Population Division reports over the recent years, such as *World Population Prospects: The 2000 Revision* (New York: United Nations, Population Division, Department of Economic and Social Affairs, 2001).
2. For a detailed probabilistic treatment of this topic, see Wolfgang Lutz, Warren Sanderson, and Sergei Scherbov, "The End of World Population Growth," *Nature* 412, August 2, 2001.
3. See UN Population Division's *World Urbanization Prospects: The 1999 Revision*. Also "2015: la ville tentaculaire," in *Libération*, November 11–12, 2000.
4. See May 23, 2000, survey on agriculture, *Economist*.
5. For an overview that also includes a historical perspective, see the UN report *Population, Environment, and Development* (New York: United Nations, 2001).

Chapter 3

1. For a wide perspective on this, see Daniel Yergin and Joseph Stanislaw (contributor), *The Commanding Heights: The Battle Between Government and the Marketplace That Is Remaking the Modern World* (New York: Simon and Schuster, 1998).
2. See Thomas L. Friedman, "A Big Stride Along the Capitalist Road to Liberty," *New York Times*, in the *International Herald Tribune*, August 13, 2001.

3. On that last point, see David Henderson, "Anti-Liberalism 2000: The Rise of the New Millennium Collectivism," Thirtieth Wincott Lecture, published by the Institute of Economic Affairs, 2001.
4. Intel Corporation recently disclosed a new structure for high-speed transistors that decreases power requirements and could put the company on course by 2007 to produce microchips with a billion transistors, twenty-five times as many as the current Pentium 4 chips. There is some evidence that Moore's law may even have been accelerating lately.
5. Prediction made in 2001 by Vice Minister Zhang Chunjing, Ministry of Information Industries.
6. See survey on cellular telephony, *Economist*, October 7, 1999.
7. Mark Turner, "The Call on Africa Grows Louder," *Financial Times*, August 21, 2001.
8. For a debate on the future of the new world economy, see *The Future of the Global Economy: Towards a Long Boom?* (Organization for Economic Cooperation and Development, 1999). Also: Michael L. Dertouzos, *What Will Be* (San Francisco: HarperEdge, 1997).

Chapter 4

1. See "Floating on Air," *Economist*, May 19, 2001.
2. Kelvin Chan, "Sewing Africa into Loop," *International Herald Tribune*, July 18, 2001.
3. For a good recent perspective by Peter Drucker on this, see his survey, "The Next Society," *Economist*, November 3, 2001.
4. Thomas Friedman, "In Ghana, Hope Arrives Via Satellite," *New York Times*, in *International Herald Tribune*, 2001.
5. Philip Evans and Thomas S. Wurster, *Blown to Bits: How the New Economics of Information Transforms Strategy* (Boston: Harvard Business School Press, 1999). Also Frances Cairncross, *The Company of the Future: How the Communications Revolution Is Changing Management* (Boston: Harvard Business School Press, 2002).
6. Regarding the increase of outsourcing of more routine internal activities, see "Out of the Back Room," *Economist*, December 1, 2001.
7. See Tony Jackson, "Plugged into the IT Revolution," in a series published in the *Financial Times* starting October 13, 1998.
8. See "They Share Horses, Don't They?" *Economist*, September 1, 2001.
9. Quote from Stan Davis and Christopher Meyer, *Blur* (New York: Warner Books, 1999).
10. "Le pneu increvable, ou la révolution façon Michelin," *Challenges*, June 2001.
11. Barbara J. Feder, "Motorola Claims Breakthrough in Specialty Chips," *New York Times*, in *International Herald Tribune*, September 15, 2001.

12. For an overview of changes in the banking sector, see "The Virtual Threat," survey in *Economist*, May 18, 2000.
13. Brad Spurgeon, "Big Brother Aside, Smart ID Cards Are Making Global Converts," *International Herald Tribune*, November 16, 2001.

Chapter 5

1. For a perceptive piece on this, see Tony Jackson, "The Eclipse of Manufacturing: Making Money from Things Is Getting Harder," *Financial Times*, December 15, 1998.
2. This can be seen from the fact that the tech correction, and the slowdown and recession it brought about, had not much to do with the U.S. Federal Reserve's raising interest rates (as the Fed often did when excess demand occurred under the old cycle). The correction had more to do with the popping of a bubble, and in that sense it resembles some much older phenomena more characteristic of the nineteenth century and the beginning of the twentieth.
3. A new study by a panel organized by the U.S. National Academy of Sciences has recently come out raising some questions on the 1997 recalculation. Even though it does not make any precise estimate as to whether the consumer price index overstates the true rate of inflation and by how much, the panel implies that the claim made in 1997 may have to be studied some more. In any case, reported inflation has now been significantly reduced through recent changes brought about by U.S. government statisticians themselves.
4. See "U.S. Productivity Rises 2.1%, Defying a Slumping Economy," *International Herald Tribune*, September 6, 2001. Also notice how even well after September 11, 2001, Alan Greenspan, the chairman of the Federal Reserve Board, has kept reaffirming his belief that technology-enabled higher productivity rates are here to stay, even if the global recession makes this temporarily harder to believe, calling the prospects for longer-term productivity growth "scarcely diminished." On this, also see Ken Rogoff and James Morsink, "Permanent Revolution: A Slump in Technology Shares Will Not Eliminate the Sector's Impact on Productivity," from the IMF research unit, in the *Financial Times*, September 21, 2001. Note that eight out of nine U.S. recessions since World War II were accompanied by plummeting productivity growth. But this was not the case for the last 2001 recession, whose downturn was mitigated by the remarkable stability of productivity growth.
5. The Larry Summers speech is quoted in the *Atlantic Monthly* of January 2001. Note his describing the negative feedback economy as a "thermostat" economy, and the positive-feedback one as an "avalanche" economy.
6. See http://www.conferenceboard.org for the recent Conference Board report on this, as well as William W. Lewis, Vincent Palmade, Baudoin

Regout, and Allen P. Webb, "What's Right with the U.S. Economy," *McKinsey Quarterly* 1 (2002).

Here's an important additional point: the positive feedback economy and the increased flexibility in the key markets may indeed explain the raising of the economy's speed limit, part of the explanation for higher productivity growth. But it may be a deep-rooted innovation process that represents the stepping on the gas pedal that propels the new world economy towards that expanded speed limit. Innovation comes in two modes: an additive mode where innovations just pile up one by one; and a multiplicative mode where a particular innovation is so basic that it triggers secondary innovations in many other areas that in turn feed back on the original invention. The latter case, referred to as a "multiplicative innovation regime," happens once in a while around general purpose technologies that go very deep—like the invention of continuous rotary motion, or binary logic. It is this last general purpose technology—binary logic forms the inner core of the new telecommunications and computer technologies that are changing everything—that may well be the force that propels the new world economy up to the now expanded speed limit, and the resulting higher productivity growth trend. On general purpose technologies, see T. Bresnahan and M. Trajtenberg, "General Purpose Technologies: Engines of Growth?" National Bureau of Economic Research Working Paper No. 4148, August 1992, discussed by Horace W. Brock in the August 1995 report of Strategic Economic Decisions (SED).

7. PEOPlink was a pioneer; others include Viatru, Virtual Souk, and so on.
8. For instance, Kevin Kelly, *New Rules for the New Economy, 10 Ways the New Economy Is Changing Everything* (London: Fourth Estate, 1998), preceded by Kevin Kelly, *Out of Control* (New York: Addison-Wesley Publishing Company, 1994), an awe-inspiring and eye-opening book. Also see Lester C. Thurow, "Building Wealth: The New Rules for Individuals, Companies, and Nations," *Atlantic Monthly*, June 1999. Or Richard T. Pasquale, Mark Millemann, and Linda Gioja, *Surfing the Chaos: The Laws of Nature and the Laws of Business* (New York: Crown Business, 2000).
9. See Robert H. Franck and Philip J. Cook, *The Winner-Take-All Society: Why the Few at the Top Get So Much More Than the Rest of Us* (New York: Martin Kessler Books at the Free Press, 1995).
10. See also Martin Wolf, "The Curse of Global Inequality," *Financial Times*, January 26, 2000.
11. Janny Scott, "1990 Boom Felt by Only a Few," *New York Times*, in the *International Herald Tribune*, 2001.
12. For a perspective on this, see Lowell Bryan and Diana Farrell, *Market Unbound* (New York: John Wiley and Sons, 1996).

13. See Alison Mitchell, "Moving to Head Off a Digital Pearl Harbor," *New York Times*, in the *International Herald Tribune*, November 20, 2001.
14. For an entertaining and insightful discussion on the difference between cretins, fools, morons, and lunatics, see Chapter 10 of Umberto Eco, *Foucault's Pendulum* (New York: Harcourt Brace Jovanovich, 1989)!
15. Also see the provoking article by Harvey Cox, "The Market as God," *Atlantic Monthly*, March 1999.

Chapter 6

1. See Michael Skapinger and Christopher Brown-Humes, "The Nordic Minnow That Took Over the Sea," in a three-part series started June 20, 2001, in the *Financial Times*.

Chapter 7

1. See, for instance, Jeffrey E. Garten, *The Mind of the CEO* (New York: Basic Books, 2001).
2. See, for example, David Berreby, "The Hunter-Gatherers of the Knowledge Economy," in *Strategy and Business*, Booz Allen and Hamilton, iss. 16, third quarter, 1999.
3. For another perspective on these issues, see Francis Fukuyama, "Death of Hierarchy," *Financial Times*, June 12–13, 1999, drawn from *The Great Disruption: Human Nature and the Reconstitution of Social Order* (New York: Simon and Schuster, 1999). The problem hierarchies face in dealing with information and controls was already addressed by Friedrich von Hayek half a century ago.
4. Although I did not show this in Figure 7.2, even the political system starts being affected by cross-border forces: Belgium, for example, has passed a "loi de compétence universelle" enabling local magistrates to judge foreign leaders for things they did at home. Similarly, a Spanish judge tried to go after Chile's Augusto Pinochet. Intervention wars (see later in Chapter 13) are another case in point.
5. For a European survey following the pattern of those made in the United States, see "Les adolescents sont indifférents à la politique, pas à la misère," *Le Monde*, March 4–5, 2001.
6. See Virginia Postrel, *The Future and Its Enemies* (New York: Free Press, 1998).
7. Historian Barry Strauss thinks that this struggle may mark the final stage in a battle between two eighteenth-century ideas. The first, the ideal of the Enlightenment, maintained that all people have an equal right to freedom, which, used productively and rationally, leads to peace and prosperity, in turn moving civilizations to a world without wars and without borders. The second built on the older Augsburg-Westphalia counter-ideal, whereby freedom can only be exercised

among one's own kind—the idea behind nationalism and nation-states, with their keenness on asserting borders. For two centuries, the world has seen a tussle between the Enlightenment ideal and its ugly twin. The outcome has been in doubt, but the two big forces are bound to tilt the advantage towards the former. Drawn from Barry Strauss, "A Truly Crucial Chapter in the History of Borders," *International Herald Tribune*, May 2, 1999.

8. Visit http://www.cisco.com/edu/academy.
9. For an intriguing personal account, see Joseph Jaworski, *Synchronicity* (San Francisco: Berrett-Koehler Publishers, 1996, 1998).
10. In a limited but telling example, a large group of companies from the power, telecommunications, transport and service sectors made public calls for the entry into force of the Kyoto Protocol. See http://www.emission55.com.
11. See Roger Lowenstein's spellbinding *When Genius Failed: The Rise and Fall of Long-Term Capital Management* (New York: Random House, 2000).
12. See Joseph S. Nye, "The Best and the Brightest Now Shun Public Service," in the *International Herald Tribune*, August 24, 2001.

Part Two

Chapter 8

1. Kevin H. O'Rourke and Jeffrey G. Williamson, *Globalization and History: The Evolution of a Nineteenth Century Atlantic Economy* (Cambridge, MA, and London: MIT, 1999).
2. Karl Polanyi, *The Great Transformation: The Political and Economic Origins of Our Time* (Boston: Beacon Press, 1957). Also around that theme: in *Globalizing Capital: A History of the International Monetary System* (Princeton: Princeton University Press, 1996), 5, Barry Eichengreen describes his own arguments as "an elaboration of the one advanced by Karl Polanyi . . . that the extension of the institutions of the market over the course of the nineteenth century aroused a political reaction in the form of associations and lobbies that ultimately undermined the stability of the market system." Another book with examples of backlash as people are affected by global changes: Thomas L. Friedman, *The Lexus and the Olive Tree: Understanding Globalization* (New York: Farrar, Straus and Giroux, 1999).
3. See Jürgen Habermas, "Die postnationale Konstellation und die Zukunft der Demokratie," in his *Die postnationale Konstellation, Politische Essays* (Frankfurt-on-Main: Suhrkamp Verlag, 1998), consulted in French

translation, "La constellation postnationale et l'avenir de la démocratie," in *Après l'Etat-nation: une nouvelle constellation politique* (Paris: Librairie Arthème Fayard, 2000).

4. See Joseph Nye and Robert Keohane, "Globalization: What's New? What's Not? (And So What?)," *Foreign Policy* 104 (Spring 2000).

Chapter 10

1. See "West Missing Emissions Targets," *Financial Times*, June 12, 2000: "The future of the 1997 Kyoto Protocol on climate change is being jeopardized by the failure of much of Europe, as well as the U.S., to curb greenhouse gas emissions." Indeed, it's not only the United States that has been increasing emissions: the Netherlands, which was supposed to cut overall emissions by 6 percent below 1990 levels by 2010, is already producing 17 percent more carbon dioxide than in 1990; emissions in Austria have increased by 13 percent.
2. See, for example, David G. Victor, "Europe's Deal to Rescue the Kyoto Protocol Rescues Nothing," *International Herald Tribune*, August 24, 2001. In February 2002, the U.S. government came up with its own plans to reduce "greenhouse gas intensity" by 18 percent over the coming decade. Greenhouse gas intensity is the ratio of greenhouse gas emissions divided by gross domestic product. But since most forecasts call for GDP to increase by some 30 percent over the period, this is tantamount to allowing a substantial increase in emissions over today's levels. Economist Paul Krugman put it bluntly: "In fact, the administration proposed to achieve almost nothing; consistent with that goal, it also announced specific policies that are trivial in scope and will have virtually no effect." See Paul Krugman, "Bush's Plan Won't Do a Thing to Halt Global Warming," *International Herald Tribune*, February 16–17, 2002.
3. Christopher D. Stone, *The Gnat Is Older Than Man: Global Environment and Human Agenda* (Princeton: Princeton University Press, 1993), 82.

Chapter 11

1. Wolfgang Reinicke has been a pioneer in this area: see his *Global Public Policy: Governing Without Government?* (Washington, DC: Brookings Institution Press, 1998), as well as Wolfgang Reinicke and Francis Deng, *Critical Choices: The United Nations, Networks, and the Future of Global Governance* (Ottawa: International Development Research Centre, 2000).
2. On another, not inconsistent classification, see Inge Kaul, Isabelle Grunberg, and Marc Stern, *Global Public Goods: International Cooperation in the 21st Century* (New York: Oxford University Press, 1999).

Chapter 12

1. In Garrett Hardin, "The Tragedy of the Commons," *Science* 162 (1968):1243.
2. Gregg Easterbrook, "Something Can Be Done About Global Warming," *International Herald Tribune*, August 30, 2001.
3. See IPCC web site at http://www.ipcc.ch. In a recent, controversial book, *The Skeptical Environmentalist* (Cambridge: Cambridge University Press, 2001), Bjørn Lomborg, a statistician from Denmark, takes a deliberate contrarian view on the global warming issue, and on other issues such as biodiversity, deforestation, fisheries depletion, water deficits, not to mention energy, food, and population. If you decide to read that book, you should also read the critical pieces on it by Stephen Schneider ("Global Warming: Neglecting the Complexities"), John P. Holdren ("Energy: Asking the Wrong Questions"), John Boongarts ("Population: Ignoring Its Impact"), and Thomas Lovejoy ("Biodiversity: Dismissing Scientific Process"), all in *Scientific American*, January 2002.
4. See, for example, Scott Wilson, "Peru's Shrinking Glaciers May Bring Disasters," *International Herald Tribune*, 2001.
5. A study recently made public by the U.S. National Academy of Sciences warns that human-induced greenhouse and other effects could increase the occurrence of the kind of very abrupt global or regional climate changes that appear to have happened at large intervals in the past. In Greenland some 11,500 years ago, temperatures shot up 8°C in less than ten years, doubling the snowfall in just three years. Similarly, the North Atlantic heated up in the 1920s, followed by persistent drought in the American West in the following decade. Conversely, temperatures dropped 6°C 8,200 years ago. See Hervé Morin, "L' évolution du climat réserve parfois des surprises inévitables," *Le Monde*, December 15, 2001.
6. See Jeremy Thomson, "Les courants océaniques, grands maîtres des changements climatiques," *Le Monde*, January 12, 2001.
7. "An Early Warning by Pacific Islands to the Mighty," by Leo A. Falcam, president of the Federated States of Micronesia, in the *International Herald Tribune*, August 16, 2001.
8. See, for example, Andre Simms, "No True Friend of the Earth," in an article that also takes exception to Lomborg's contrarian views, in the *International Herald Tribune*, Fall 2001.
9. See the comprehensive report *Fuel for Thought,* World Bank, 2000; and Amory B. Lovins and L. Hunter Lovins, "Climate Change: Making Sense and Making Money," Rocky Mountain Institute, 1997. Also José Goldemberg, "For a Less Vulnerable Energy System, Switch to Renewables," *International Herald Tribune*, Fall 2001.

10. For several other ideas, see Vanessa Houlder, "Down-to-Earth Plans for Carbon Dioxide," *Financial Times*, November 9, 2001.
11. These means include letting firms trade carbon emission credits (that is, if a firm does better than its ceiling, it gets a credit that another firm can buy to help it meet its own ceiling), doing away with at least some of the world's huge energy subsidies (which cost governments huge amounts, never reach the poor, and kill prospects for de-carbonization), and going all-out in providing incentives for technological research, applications, and sharing.
12. See Robert T. Watson et al., "Protecting Our Planet, Securing Our Future" (Washington, DC: UNEP, U.S. National Aeronautics and Space Administration, World Bank, 1998), World Bank Working Paper 20757, 18. See also Henry Gee, "Comment freiner l'extinction annoncée des espèces vivantes?" *Le Monde*, March 10, 2000.
13. Some, like the World Conservation Union (IUCN), say that it's one in four. See Note 17 below on *IUCN Red List*.
14. Carol Kaesuk Yoon, "Another Bad Year for Penguins," *New York Times*, in the *International Herald Tribune*, June 28, 2001.
15. *World Resources 2000–2001 (People and Ecosystems: The Fraying Web of Life)*, UNDP, UNEP, World Bank, World Resources Institute, 2000.
16. Also see Norman Myers and Crispin Tickell, "Cutting Evolution Down to Our Size," *Financial Times*, October 27–28, 2001; and William Souder, "A Sneak Preview of Earth 2050: The Study of Plant Species Makes a Case for Biodiversity," *Washington Post*, in the *International Herald Tribune*, April 19, 2001, referring to a study by a University of Minnesota team led by Peter Reich.
17. The World Conservation Union (IUCN) believes that a major conservation drive would require 10 to 100 times today's level of spending. See the IUCN's *2000 Red List of Threatened Species*.
18. See Guy Gugliotta, "Tiny Lizard Illustrates Big Lessons on Habitat," *Washington Post*, December 3, 2001.
19. "Hard Facts, Hidden Problems: A Review of Current Data on Fishing Subsidies," WWF International, see http://www.panda.org.
20. See Joshua Reichert, "If the Sea Lion Starves, Pity the Fishing Fleets," *International Herald Tribune*, October 17, 2000.
21. See "Fishy Figures," *Economist*, December 1, 2001.
22. See "Net Benefits," *Economist*, February 24, 2001.
23. See "Economic Man, Cleaner Planet," *Economist*, September 29, 2001.
24. See *World Resources 2000–2001*, Note 15 above.
25. Information collected by the London-based Environmental Investigation Agency and its Indonesian partner, Telapak.
26. See Thomas Lovejoy, "Biodiversity: Dismissing Scientific Process," *Scientific American*, January 2002 issue.

27. For an example on the Amazonian rain forest, see "Managing the Rainforests," *Economist*, May 12, 2001. On certification of sustainability in general, see Jared Diamond, "Finding Value in the Environment," *International Herald Tribune*, January 12, 2000.
28. "Le lac Tchad en voie de disparition," *Sciences et Avenir*, April 2001.
29. See Philip Ball, "Running on Empty: The World Is Dangerously Short of Water and a Global Crisis Could Be Just 20 Years Away," *Financial Times*, October 2–3, 1999. The sharing of the Jordan River (and of the aquifers) is a serious long-term issue in the Middle East.
30. In China, the Beijing aquifer is seriously threatened and many rivers have stopped flowing, with an exceptional drought making things worse. Prime Minister Zhu Rongji went as far as to say, in spring 2001, that "water shortage is a serious obstacle to China's economic and social development." See "Une sécheresse exceptionelle accélère la désertification du nord de la Chine," *Le Monde*, August 18, 2001. Even rich countries can face major threats to their further development: Malaysia has recently had to start thinking about reducing its supply of water to Singapore.
31. Visit http://www.nilebasin.org.
32. In French cities, life expectancy went from 32 years to 45 years between 1850 and 1900 as they implemented big improvements in water supply and wastewater disposal. It's this kind of success that now needs replicating in much of the developing world.
33. According to the World Commission on Water.
34. The International Maritime Organization, or IMO, is small, severely budget-constrained (only $26 million a year), and under scrutiny. See Michael Peel and Francesco Guerrera, "Sea Change for International Shipping Body: The UN Agency Has Had a Low Profile Since It First Met in 1959," *Financial Times*, August 21, 2001. A recent example of lax enforcement: under a North Atlantic convention, France was supposed to cut by half the quantity of nitrates emitted into the ocean; instead, it doubled it between 1985 and 1999, to 375,000 tons per year.

Chapter 13

1. Martin Wolf, "The View from the Limousine," *Financial Times*, November 7, 2001. A similar image has been used by Robert Kaplan in the *Atlantic Monthly*. Recent data show that the world's richest 50 million people earn as much as the poorest 2.7 billion.
2. For an overview, see World Bank, *World Development Report 2000–2001: Attacking Poverty* (Oxford: Oxford University Press, 2001).
3. To put this in perspective: that's one out of five people on earth, compared to three out of four in 1820. See World Bank, *Globalization, Growth and Poverty* (Oxford: Oxford University Press, 2002).

4. See Sylvie Brunel, *La faim dans le monde* (Paris: Presses Universitaires de France, 1999).
5. See Deepa Narayan et al., World Bank, *Voices of the Poor,* 3 vols. (Oxford: Oxford University Press, 2000–2002).
6. For example, increases in inequality in different Thai provinces have substantially offset the potential for poverty reduction based on growth. At the national level, inequality in income distribution increased in Thailand at the end of the 1990s, pushing an additional 2 million people into poverty. See World Bank, "Thailand Social Monitor: Poverty and Public Policy," November 2001. See also chapter 5.
7. See above-mentioned *World Development Report 2000–2001*, as well as Vinod Thomas et al., *The Quality of Growth* (Oxford: Oxford University Press, 2000).
8. Resolution No. 2626 adopted by the General Assembly of the UN on October 24, 1970.
9. See World Bank, *Assessing Aid: What Works, What Doesn't and Why* (Oxford: Oxford University Press, 2000); and C. Burnside and David Dollar, "Aid, Policies and Growth," *American Economic Review* 86 (2) (2000).
10. How important a good business climate is can be seen from the experience of India. In those of its states that are least successful in fighting poverty, entrepreneurs face costs significantly higher than in other states. Indian entrepreneurs perceive an overall cost saving of 30 percent between the best and worst states, a large competitive disadvantage for firms to overcome.
11. See Nitin Desai and Jayantha Dhanapala, "A Peace Dividend for Developing Countries Would Pay Off," *International Herald Tribune*, Fall 2000.
12. Suggested among others by John Ruggie, professor at Harvard's Kennedy School of Government in "UN Peacekeepers Are No Quick Fix for Afghanistan," *International Herald Tribune*, October 27–28, 2001.
13. For a perspective on this topic, see "Why and when to Go In," *Economist*, January 6, 2001. Former U.S. president Jimmy Carter has deplored the "peace making vacuum" in "As a Peacemaker, America Is Blundering Badly," *International Herald Tribune*, May 28, 1999.
14. Paul Collier, "Economic Causes of Civil Conflict and Their Implications for Policy," World Bank, June 15, 2000.
15. See, for example, R. Nicholas Burns, "NATO Is Vital for the Challenges of the Next Century," *International Herald Tribune*, November 10–11, 2001; and Jackson Diehl, "Big Plans for a Fraying Atlantic Alliance in Need of a Mission," *International Herald Tribune*, November 13, 2001. Some have suggested another track: Graham Allison, Karl Kaiser, and

Sergei Karaganov, "The World Needs a Global Alliance for Security," *International Herald Tribune*, November 21, 2001.

16. Robert J. Barro, "Human Capital and Growth," *American Economic Review* 91 (2): 12–17.
17. See "L' accréditation des compétences dans la société cognitive," proceedings from a conference held in February 1998, edited by J. L. Reiffers (France: Éditions de l'Aube, 1998).
18. The influenza virus that killed some 20 million people during the "Spanish" flu pandemic of 1918–1919 was recently traced to swine. According to findings published in *Science* in 2001, researchers were able to reconstruct the DNA of the virus after discovering a female patient buried in the Alaskan permafrost; the virus turned out to be a hybrid between pig and human influenzas.
19. You'll find a good overview in "The Urgency of a Massive Effort Against Infectious Diseases," statement by David L. Heynmann, WHO, before the Committee on International Relations, U.S. House of Representatives, June 29, 2000.
20. I use "AIDS" as a shortcut descriptor, even where the more precise term should be "HIV and AIDS."
21. See Mark Derr, "New Theories on the Black Death," *New York Times*, in the *International Herald Tribune*, October 4, 2001.
22. See Murray Feshbach, "Dead Souls," *Atlantic Monthly*, January 1999.
23. Regarding AIDS in Asia more generally, see "Sex Bomb: The Struggle Against AIDS in Asia Is Far from Over," *Economist*, October 6, 2001.
24. Nicol Degli Innocenti, "AIDS Named as South Africa's Biggest Killer," *Financial Times*, 2001, quoting a report by the country's Medical Research Council.
25. See the tragic case of Zimbabwe in Mark Turner, "The Shadow of AIDS Is Casting a Pall of Darkness over the Heart of Africa," *Financial Times*, July 1, 2000.
26. More because a substantial upgrade of the developing countries' health systems is in any case called for. See a commentary on a recent WHO report (Jeffrey Sachs et al.) recommending just that: Martin Wolf, "The Low Cost of Better Health," *Financial Times*, January 9, 2002. The report itself: "Macroeconomics and Health: Investing in Health for Economic Development" (Geneva: WHO, 2001). The developing countries would need additional aid of about $25 billion to achieve this.
27. See the fascinating Laurie Garrett, *Betrayal of Trust: The Collapse of Global Public Health* (New York: Hyperion, 2000). Many of the remarkable, pioneering global public health advances of New York City between 1890 and 1920 have not only failed to take hold a century later, but we have failed to build the equivalent approach at the level

of the planet. This approach made stronger scientific and political links between germs and infectious diseases than are made today and focused in a pragmatic way on the interests of the New York community as a whole, providing proteins to tenement dwellers, food inspections, disease surveillance, and epidemic control for all, pure water, clean streets, improved housing, and safer streets. In a way, the whole world is becoming like New York City, but global thinking hasn't caught up with this.

28. You could add to this an altogether different angle: the need to kick up, after September 11, 2001, unprecedented efforts aimed at countering biological weapons. Here's how urgent this is: a 1972 convention on biological weapons was readily ignored by Moscow, which at the peak in the late 1990s employed 60,000 people at producing thousands of tons of anthrax, smallpox, and plague. There were even some experiments suggesting an intention to combine ebola and smallpox into a terribly lethal weapon and to make biological weapons treatment-resistant. This covert program was discontinued in 1992, but there's no telling what leftovers may be circulating around in the world, which still counts six producing countries at this time.
29. See "Information Infrastructure Indicators, 1990–2010" in the info*Dev* web site http://www.infodev.org.
30. See J. F. Rischard, "Connecting Developing Countries to the Information Technology Revolution," *SAIS Review* (Winter–Spring 1996). There is a lot of information about real and potential applications in the just-mentioned info*Dev* web site. Also see Miria A. Pigato, "Information and Communication Technology, Poverty, and Development in Sub-Saharan Africa and South Asia," World Bank, Africa Region Working Paper No. 20. For a short overview: "A Great Leap," *Time*, January 31, 2001.

Chapter 14

1. See "The Mystery of the Vanishing Taxpayer," survey in the *Economist*, January 29, 2000.
2. Since cross-border financial flows are enormous (more than a trillion dollars a day), a small tax could yield large proceeds; not so for international arm sales, which, after going up three years in a row to 2000, reached $36 billion in that year.
3. See, for instance, George Kopits, "Solving a Taxing Problem," *Financial Times*, June 5, 2000.
4. A recent disagreement between the EU and the United States vividly illustrates the consequences of the lack of such a global approach. It relates to the first, new world economy–related strand: EU finance ministers have agreed to levy a tax, for three years, on EU residents that

download music, software, and computer games through the Internet. The United States, by contrast, is wary of any such tax at this time.

5. The difference between therapeutic and reproductive cloning is not that clear-cut, as could be seen from the reaction to the announcement on November 25, 2001, by the Massachusetts company Advanced Cell Technology that it had cloned the first human embryo. Yet the company was not trying to create a human being (reproductive cloning), but just an embryo from which it could collect stem cells (therapeutic cloning). All the embryos died out, and it is unclear whether the company got the eggs to produce any new cells. Nonetheless, for a few hours, the test tubes contained the first makings of a human life. See "The Politics of Cloning," *Economist*, December 1, 2001.
6. Robert Kuttner, "A Global Market Isn't As Easy As It Looks," *Business Week*, September 3, 2001.
7. The Bank of England and the Bank of Canada even launched a paper recently that argues for strict limits on IMF bailouts, to compel countries to face debt crises earlier. See http://www.bankofengland.co.uk.
8. Some finance ministers had begun to allude to the idea of a Chapter 11-like process for crisis countries, but the real surprise came from a Washington speech alluding to the idea by Anne Krueger, the IMF's deputy managing director, late in November 2001. See "When Countries Go Bust," *Economist*, December 8, 2001. The U.S. Secretary of the Treasury had supported the idea already months before, and since Anne Krueger's speech, several other G7 and non-G7 countries have expressed broad support, pending a more detailed formulation of the legal aspects, some of which will be very tricky. There would in effect be three phases, as described by economist Jeffrey Sachs, one of the early proponents of this idea: first, the country would receive temporary protection from its creditors; then, as debt negotiations proceeded, creditors that put in new money would receive seniority over others; finally, once debt negotiation was agreed, majority voting would stop dissenters from objecting. The last aspect is particularly problematic from a legal standpoint, particularly for holders of existing bonds whose clauses did not specifically allow for this. To complicate things, some NGOs claim that Chapter 9 rather than Chapter 11 is the more relevant model.
9. Rebuilding the International Financial Architecture," EMEPG Seoul Report, October 2001; and Stephany Griffith-Jones, Jenny Kimmis, and Ariel Buria, "The Reform of Global Financial Arrangements," Institute of Development Studies, report prepared for the Commonwealth Secretariat, 2001.

10. For a good overview of financial crises, see "World Economic Outlook," May 1998, IMF, chap. 4.
11. Formulating such principles is one area where there has been progress since 1997–1998, under the constant prodding of British Chancellor of the Exchequer Gordon Brown. The IMF, the World Bank, and the OECD, sometimes working with international professional associations, have started to formulate broad codes for bank supervision, monetary policy-making, corporate governance, and so on, but for some, like corporate governance, it's still early days.
12. "Shining a Light on a Company's Accounts," *Economist*, August 18, 2001. Unbelievably, at the same time, Japanese banks are allowed to pile up large exposures to swaps and other derivatives without having to disclose them to investors; see "Storing Up Trouble," *Economist*, August 25, 2001.
13. "The Latest Bubble?" *Economist*, September 1, 2001.
14. See Joseph Stiglitz and Leif Pagrotsky, "Blocking the Terrorists' Funds," *Financial Times*, December 7, 2001.
15. See Michael Klein, "Banks Lose Control of Money," *Financial Times*, January 14, 2000.
16. Michael Richardson, "Singapore Faces Big Adjustments," *Financial Times*, October 26, 2001.
17. See Jeffrey E. Garten, "Beware of the Weak Links in Our Globalization Chain," op-ed in the *New York Times*, in the *International Herald Tribune*, 1999.
18. See "The World Geopolitics of Drugs," Annual Report of the Observatoire Géopolitique des Drogues, April 2000; *World Drug Report 2000* (UN Office for Drug Control and Crime Prevention, 2000); *Global Illicit Drug Trends 2001* (UN ODCCP, 2001); and the very comprehensive "High Time" survey of illegal drugs in the *Economist*, July 28, 2001, from which I have drawn quite a bit.
19. Richard Labévière, *Les dollars de la terreur* (Paris: Bernard Grasset, 1999).
20. See "L' école de la deuxième chance de Marseille à la lumière des experiences internationales," proceedings from a 1997 conference in Marseille, ed. J. L. Reiffers (Éditions de l'Aube, 1997); and *The Second Chance: Learning in the Context of the Second Chance School Pilot Scheme* (Brussels: European Commission, March 2001).
21. See the above-mentioned *Globalization, Growth, and Poverty*, World Bank, 2002.
22. Paraphrasing U.S. Secretary of State Colin Powell in a *Wall Street Journal* op-ed, Fall 2001.
23. And Russia is waiting in the wings. It is the only major power left outside the WTO, and momentum is building behind its bid for entry after

the November 2001 summit meeting between George Bush and Vladimir Putin in the United States.

24. In 1998, OECD countries paid out $360 billion in agricultural support. The highest rates of support are for milk, rice, and sugar producers. Producer support as a percentage of farm receipts was 60, 40, and 20 percent in Japan, the EU, and the United States, respectively. See May 23, 2000, survey in the *Economist*.
25. See Ministerial Declaration, WTO, Ministerial Conference, Fourth Session, Doha, November 9–14, 2001, dated November 14, 2001.
26. Visit UNCTAD web site at http://www.unctad.org. Also see Reginald Dale, "Global Investment Needs New Rules," *International Herald Tribune*, October 2000.
27. Jeffrey E. Garten, "As Business Goes Global, Antitrust Should, Too," *Business Week*, November 13, 2000.
28. See the crystal-clear piece "Market for Ideas," *Economist*, April 14, 2001, from which this way of describing the basic issue is drawn.
29. "Polémique autour de la brevetabilité du logiciel," *Le Monde*, September 12, 2001.
30. See Adriana Eunjung Cha, "Free Software Makes Inroads into the Microsoft Empire," *Washington Post*, in the *International Herald Tribune*, 2001.
31. See Patti Waldmeir, "Laws of Contradiction," *Financial Times*, Fall 2001.
32. "Crops and Robbers: How Patents Jeopardize Global Food Security," Action Aid, 2001.
33. See "Life Story," survey in the *Economist*, June 29, 2000.
34. See Donald G. McNeil Jr., "Demand for Antibiotic May Alter U.S. Patent Policies," *New York Times,* in the *International Herald Tribune*, October 18, 2001.
35. The "seventh continent" expression has been attributed to the CEO of Intel.
36. See "Shopping Around the Web," survey in the *Economist*, February 24, 2000, and "We Have Lift-Off," *Economist*, February 3, 2001.
37. "Ignore French Website Ruling, Says US Judge," *Financial Times*, November 7, 2001.
38. A solution has recently emerged: "geolocation" software that attempts to match a person's location based on a computers' Internet (IP) address. If this worked, this could bring an answer to the logjam problem between conflicting country laws, as access could then be denied to residents of this or that country for this or that legal reason specific to that country. But this would Balkanize the Internet in damageable ways (forcing among other things all web site operators to know the

applicable laws from Andorra to Zimbabwe), and people could use other software to cloud their identities. So the jury is still out on this. See Adriana Eunjung Cha, "Bye-bye Borderless Web: Countries Are Raising Electronic Fences," *Washington Post*, in the *International Herald Tribune*, January 5–6, 2001.

39. See "Stop Signs on the Web," *Economist*, January 13, 2001.
40. See Thomas L. Friedman, "The Real Threat Is Cyberterrorism," *New York Times,* in the *International Herald Tribune*, Fall 2001, and Thorold Baker, "Cybercrime Threat to E-Business," *Financial Times*, Fall 2001.
41. Gina Kolata, "Stealth Messages on Internet Leave No Outward Evidence," *New York Times*, October 2001, and "Des messages terroristes peuvent se cacher dans les images de la toile," *Le Monde*, September 21, 2001. It's an old technique: Herodotus describes how a message tattooed on a slave's skull and covered by subsequent hair growth gave the signal for a rebellion against the Persians.
42. See, for example, Robert Taylor, "Breaking the Bonds of Forced Labor," *Financial Times*, December 10, 2001.
43. For an example of this line of thinking, see IILS Public Lecture on "Work, Empowerment and Equality," by Cambridge professor Bob Hepple, on the ILO web site http://www.ilo.org.
44. For instance, Maria Nowak in "Pour le droit à l'initiative économique," *Le Monde*, December 11, 1998.
45. These and other ideas around "decent work" have been promoted mostly by Juan Somavia, the current director-general of the ILO.
46. See Kimberly Ann Elliott, "The ILO and Enforcement of Core Labor Standards," Institute of International Economics (IIE), July 2000, updated April 2001, on the IIE web site http://www.iie.com.
47. See "Break the Link Between Trade and Labor," by professor Jagdish Bhagwati, in the *Financial Times*, August 29, 2001.
48. Samuel Huntington, "Migration Flows Are the Central Issue of Our Time," *International Herald Tribune*, September 2001.
49. For a recent piece on immigration issues, see Jonathan Coppel et al., "Trends in Immigration and Economic Consequences," Economics Department Working Paper 284, June 2001, OECD.
50. Most current national immigration policies are designed to keep people out, not to facilitate their coming in. See Dani Rodrik, "Mobilising the World's Labor Assets," *Financial Times*, December 12, 2001.
51. Nicol Degli Innocenti, "Virus Hits at the Country Life Force," *Financial Times*, September 26, 2001.
52. Sharing the Spoils: Taxing International Human Capital Flows," June 2001, preliminary working draft by Mihir Desai, Devesh Kapur, and John McHale, all three from Harvard University.

Part Three

Chapter 15

1. An economists' concept called "global public goods" has recently begun to invade this fledging field and, while helpful in some ways, has in some other ways done damage, mostly by turning people off through classifications founded on abstract categories and jargon rather than on pragmatic inventorying. Also, the underlying "goods" caption has distracted many from the real question, which is the *methodology* of global problem-solving, and focused them prematurely on aspects such as the "financing of global public goods"—important but secondary to the question of how you get to decisions in the first place.
2. "Lori's War," *Foreign Policy* 54 (Spring 2000).

Chapter 16

1. The main ideas in Chapters 16 to 21 have been laid out in J. F. Rischard, "We Need New Approaches to Global Problem-Solving, Fast," *Journal of International Economic Law* 4 (3) (September 2001); this article was based on a speech I gave on June 28, 2000, at the ABCDE-Europe Conference in Paris, and on other predecessor speeches. Also see J. F. Rischard, "A Crisis of Complexity and Global Governance," *International Herald Tribune*, October 2, 1998.
2. See Michael Richardson, "Fishing Fleets Are Raiding Ever-Remoter Seas," *International Herald Tribune*, December 31, 2001.
3. See Linda Starke, ed., *State of the World 2001* (Washington: Worldwatch Institute Books, W. W. Norton & Company, 2001).
4. See, for example, Ivo H. Daalder and James M. Lindsay, "Unilateralism Is Alive and Well in Washington," *International Herald Tribune*, December 21, 2001.
5. See Eric Pianin, "Climate Pact Marks a Victory for Europe But Russia and Others Win Concessions," *Washington Post,* in the *International Herald Tribune*, November 12, 2001.
6. Another cause for concern is that too many outfits and groups can crowd around an issue susceptible to treaty making, creating a superficial impression of activity and progress, when in fact the issue isn't being tackled in a convincing, unified way. You would be hard pressed to find a comprehensive description of the issue of rethinking taxation, yet at the same time, you have many cooks in the kitchen: the OECD's fiscal affairs committee, the IMF and the World Bank's public management and taxation practices, the Committee of International Organizations on Tax Administration (CIOTA), the UN Ad-Hoc Group of Éxperts on International Cooperation in Tax Matters, the

OECD's Global Forum on Taxation, and a recently launched Global Tax Network. On top of this, a group of wisemen tasked by the UN has proposed in 2001 to create an International Tax Organization, or ITO. Each group, each task force or forum is useful in itself, but the whole is less than the parts. You'll find this syndrome—which can also include turf fights between institutions, and an unbelievable number of meetings, papers, studies, and communiqués—around quite a few of the twenty issues. This is one of the reasons I spared you a detailed issue-by-issue description of all the world's mostly unimpressive attempts at tackling them, which would at best have given you the impression that more is happening than is actually the case.

7. University of Toronto G8 Research Group, "From G7 to G8," on the G8 Information Centre web site, http://www.g7.utoronto.ca (as of June 2001).
8. Besides participants like Britain, the United States, and France, many countries with smaller economies were invited in: the Netherlands, Luxembourg, Iceland, Liberia, Haiti, and Iran, to mention just a few. See Devish Kapur, John P. Lewis, and Richard Webb, *The World Bank: Its First Half Century*, vol. 1 (Washington, DC: Brookings Institution Press, 1997), 62.
9. Edward Bernstein to the author in 1995.
10. Professor John Kirton, "What Is the G20?" on the G8 Information Centre web site, http://www.g7.utoronto.ca (as of June 2001).
11. See, for example, Michael Hardt and Antonio Negri, "The New Faces in Genoa Want a Different Future," *International Herald Tribune*, July 25, 2001.

Chapter 17

1. Habermas makes this point in the book referenced in Note 3, Chap. 8.

Chapter 18

1. Two years ago, a search on the worldwide web under the code word "networked governance" brought only a few hits. Today, you get pages and pages of hits and the concept, originally used only by a few of us (foremost Wolfgang Reinicke, see note 1, Chapter 11), has spread and taken on several meanings. The way I use it in this book refers mainly to the question of inherently global issues and of how to accelerate their solution.

Chapter 19

1. Just to give an order of magnitude, a global issues network's membership would be in the 10^1 in the first phase, 10^2 in the second, and 10^3

in the third. The electronic town meeting companion of each network could easily enlist participants in the 10^4. The independent expert panel adjunct would enlist 10^2.

2. Given the importance of knowledge, it would be crucial that the global multilateral that becomes the lead facilitator be the one possessing the most advanced staff expertise, knowledge, and organization with respect to the global issue in question—not just some sort of proprietary claims on the issue. See J. F. Rischard, "Multilateral Development Banks and Global Public Networks: Speculations for the Next Century," *EIB Papers* 3 (2) (1998).
3. Professor Samuel Bowles pointed me to this basic finding during a discussion at the Santa Fe Institute. Ernst Fehr and Simon Gächter are among the main researchers who have investigated this topic; many of their articles are available on the worldwide web.
4. See "Regulating the Internet: The Consensus Machine," *Economist*, June 10, 2000; as well as the discussions on consensus and governance posted on the web site of the Harvard University Law School's Berkman Center for Internet and Society, http://cyber.law.harvard.edu/is99/governance/consensus.html (visited June 11, 2001)—especially the interviews with Joe Sims and John Perry Barlow.
5. For a view at variance with this one, see Michael Prowse's musings in "It's Not Who Decides, but How Well They Do It," *Financial Times*, October 27–28, 2001.
6. For a typology of these setups, see Anne-Marie Slaughter, "Global Government Networks, Global Information Agencies, and Disaggregated Democracy," Harvard Law School, Public Law Working Paper No. 18.
7. Possible but more far-fetched: in the case of some of the twenty issues, the network could even issue some norms for civil society players, for example, encouraging environmental NGOs, whose communities are troubled by egotism and frequent disagreements on what's really important, to come up with some sort of priorities map.
8. See http://www.iso.ch.

Chapter 20

1. The global issues network concept has links to what is called global public policy networks (GPPNs), but the GPPN concept has come to include all sorts of issues that are not "inherently global" in the sense suggested in this book. The global issues network concept is only for inherently global issues, and it gyrates around collective norms distillation—whereas the GPPN universe will also contain, say, regional efforts on vaccines without any element of norm production. Actually,

the GPPN concept is a broader concept that stands mostly for tri-sector partnerships these days, that is, partnerships among public sector, business, and civil society parties. In that sense, GINs, and their peculiar methodology, are a subclass of GPPNs. See Reinicke and Deng, referenced in Note 1, Chap. 11.

2. See source under Note 3, Chap. 8. Habermas's vision of "domestic policy," however, pivots around the aim of equitable redistribution, which in his view should also be the primary aim of European and global policy.
3. Ibid.
4. A distinction often pointed to by Wolfgang Reinecke, referenced in Note 1, Chap. 11.

Chapter 21

1. Jamie Carnie, referred to in *Après l'État-nation*, referenced in Note 3, Chap. 8.
2. Besides these main answers, there is another more tentative one to add for the sake of completeness: in keeping with the aim of representing plural points of view, and under the open concept of networked governance, multiple networks could emerge. Although highly unlikely, two rival networks could conceivably offer competing sets of norms for a single issue, in the same way as there are several world boxing federations. Countries and other players would then have a choice. Eventually, one network would dominate, with reputational effects as the main determinant. This situation is unlikely if only because it would be contentious: people would have to recognize which of the two networks is doing the best job in the interest of global citizenship and which has gone somewhat off track.
3. Professor Walter Fontana pointed this book out to me after a discussion at the Santa Fe Institute. See Christopher Alexander, *Notes on the Synthesis of Form* (Cambridge: Harvard University Press, 1964).

Chapter 22

1. Note that the G20 has expressed a desire to also deal with other economic issues, such as the price of oil, as early as at its Ottawa meeting at the end of October 2000. See Laurence Caramel, "Nord-Sud, Sud-Nord," *Le Monde*, November 14, 2000.
2. For source, see Note 2, Chap. 11.
3. Richard Falk and Andrew Strauss, "Toward Global Parliament," *Foreign Affairs* (January/ February 2001).
4. An idea of Jacques Delors, which recently was promoted by a UN panel that also included ex-president of Mexico Zedillo.

5. On a proposal for a G16, see Jeffrey Sachs, "Making It Work," *Economist*, as early as September 12, 1998; for replacing the G7 with a G20, see Klaus Schwab, "The World's New Actors Need a Bigger Stage," *Newsweek*, July 30, 2001.
6. In an open letter published in September 2001, Belgian Prime Minister Guy Verhofstadt proposed that the G7 be expanded to include, besides Russia, representatives of regional trading areas like East Asia's ASEAN and Latin America's Mercosur.
7. "La gouvernance mondiale," *Luxemburger Wort*, October 27, 2001. Michel Camdessus is associated with this idea.

Chapter 23

1. Chap. 21 of the already mentioned *The Great Transformation*, see under Note 2, Chap. 8. Another quote comes to mind: Shakespeare's wonderful "There is a tide in the affairs of men, which, taken at the flood, leads on to fortune" (*Julius Caesar,* IV, 111, 217).

Acknowledgments

Ten dear friends, who will recognize themselves, gave some of their free time to help me with pointers, warnings and precious fillips of encouragement along the way. I cannot thank them enough, although I remain solely responsible for the basic ideas in this book, and for any errors or instances of faulty reasoning.

Next, I have a deep debt of gratitude to the World Bank. I am not speaking here in its name, and put the book together on my own and on my own time. Yet my very ability to write this kind of book comes in part from my years in this great, open-minded, knowledge-laden institution. Contrary to what many people think, it's a place where ideas are constantly debated, half like in a squabbling faculty, and half as part of the "damned-if-you-do, damned-if-you-don't" choices that keep coming up among people committed to the daunting and complex job of fighting poverty. My deep thanks in particular to Bank President Jim Wolfensohn for always giving new ideas and even maverick ways the right amount of play. And a quiet thought for his predecessor Lew Preston, who once gave me a big push forward.

Finally, my greatest debt is to my wife, Jaqueline, for her support and patience, particularly for dealing with my virtual absence and real absent-mindedness during so many shot evenings, weekends, and holidays, when I was toiling on the book on top of my usual workload.

Index